FROM LAW SCHOOL TO LAW PRACTICE

The New Associate's Guide

American Law Institute
American Bar Association
Committee on Continuing
Professional Education

ALI ABA

4025 Chestnut Street, Philadelphia, Pennsylvania 19104

FROM LAW SCHOOL TO LAW PRACTICE

The New Associate's Guide

Suzanne B. O'Neill

and

Catherine Gerhauser Sparkman

ALI ABA

American Law Institute-American Bar Association
Committee on Continuing Professional Education
4025 Chestnut Street • Philadelphia • Pennsylvania 19104

Library of Congress Catalog Number: 89-080201

Second Printing 1989

Printed in the United States of America

ISBN: 0-8318-0593-5

Sharon T. Walsh of the ALI-ABA staff supervised the production of this book

Acknowledgments

Numerous partners, associates, and clients of law firms have related their respective expectations – of one another and specifically of new firm associates – to us during the past two years. Again, we thank them for their insight, interest, and support of this project. We also wish to memorialize our appreciation of special ongoing contributions that the following colleagues made to this effort: Chuck Billings of Vial, Hamilton, Koch & Knox in Dallas; Allen Sparkman of Davis, Graham & Stubbs in Denver; Leslie Cleveland, General Counsel and Vice President of Click and Geddes Lumber Company; Cecil Hedger of the Denver office of Heron, Burchette, Ruckert & Rothwell; A. Bruce Fishman, Chief Financial Officer of Ocean Pacific Images, Inc.; Jack Trigg of Hall & Evans in Denver; and Lauren Starnes Duncan of Annie Laurie Productions, Ltd., for her thought-provoking editing of the manuscript as it evolved. We also appreciate the helpful suggestions and support in this project that we received from Sharon Walsh, Director of the ALI-ABA Office of Books; Professor Richard Diebold Lee, founding Director of AILTO; and Mark Mendenhall, former Staff Director of AILTO.

Foreword

This volume is the first product developed under the auspices of the American Law Institute for Law Training within the Office — or, as it is known by its acronym, "AILTO." AILTO is a project of the American Law Institute-American Bar Association Committee on Continuing Professional Education, with which the American Bar Association is cooperating. It provides assistance and support to the in-house training efforts of law firms, corporate legal departments, and government agencies nationwide. Founded in 1985, AILTO embodies ALI-ABA's continuing commitment to the professional development of new lawyers. The volume was the inspiration of its co-author, Suzanne O'Neill.

Among the major changes in the legal profession over the last thirty years, perhaps the most radical has been the growth of the large firm. Firms have expanded into state-wide, regional, national, and international organizations. Satellite offices of some firms are, or are on their way to becoming, large offices in their own right. The impact of this development upon the career paths of practitioners has been of major significance.

The common goal of most law school graduates who

choose to practice is to obtain a position with a growing firm, and in due time to attain partnership status. But many have little idea what will be expected of them in the firm setting. Those who have worked as summer associates may have some insight, but even among them many will have been given limited tasks and will not have been exposed to the demands of dealing directly with clients, working for a number of different attorneys, and meeting multiple deadlines.

To fill this void, the authors of *From Law School to Law Practice: The New Associate's Guide* have produced a book that introduces the fledgling associates to exactly what they are getting into in their new environment. The handbook is aimed primarily at beginning associates, providing the insights they need to adjust quickly to the demands and expectations of their employers, to perform well from the outset, and to make the positive impression that will set them on the proper path for success in the firm. The seeds of long-term professional development can be sown early with the aid of the authors' advice.

Law firms who make this handbook available to their associates will be rewarded with a speedier adjustment to practice by their associates.

Students who read this handbook will gain an insight into what they have to look forward to — information that can also enable them to judge the firms they consider joining and to improve their chances of eliciting appropriate information about various firms, information that indicates how they will fit in and how good their opportunities will be for advancement.

ALI-ABA is grateful to Suzanne O'Neill and Catherine Gerhauser Sparkman for unselfishly sharing their expertise and experience in this area with the bar, with recent graduates, and with law students.

PAUL A. WOLKIN
Executive Director
American Law Institute-American Bar Association
Committee on Continuing Professional Education

January 30, 1989

Contents

Introducing the Pieces: Beginning this Career

A new lawyer's charge is to become an effective lawyer: to produce excellent legal work and to provide client service. The capability to produce excellent legal work is the product of law school; the ability to deliver quality client service is learned outside the structure of case studies. Excellent client service requires, in addition, an understanding of clients' expectations, professional judgment, and client relations skills. Development of each requires time and direction.

Supervising attorneys and clients have various expectations of each other and of junior associate lawyers. Understanding these expectations is a crucial component of successful orientation to the firm; it is also the first step to becoming integrated into the firm. These expectations are reflected in the often unspoken criteria of performance evaluations, including: cost-effective and timely production of work product, effective oral and written communication, practical judgment and sound decision-making, acceptance of responsibility and initiative, client relations skills, team attitude, cooperation, and ability to handle a workload.

The purpose of this book is to give new associate lawyers some practical insight and direction in addressing these expectations and to serve as a ready reference and reminder as experience, responsibilities, and client contacts increase. As new lawyers become responsive to the expectations expressed by supervising attorneys and clients, they can significantly reduce those write-downs, or write-offs, of excess hours that otherwise are expected to occur and do occur.

Part I acquaints new lawyers with the kinds of client expectations that client-oriented lawyers encounter. As associates are assigned more specialized work, fewer opportunities arise for them to handle small transactions or disputes and to spend non-billable time observing experienced firm members as part of their training. Working on projects that come to them only in piecemeal fashion, new associates are faced with difficulties in developing a sense of the client's goals, businesses, and expectations in large matters. For example, these expectations include assumptions that the attorney will:

- understand what the client wants to do;
- communicate progress and status;

- be accessible and return calls promptly;
- use economic sense; and
- understand a corporate law department's expectations.

A new lawyer's immediate clients are supervising attorneys. Focusing consistently on the expectations of supervising attorneys, charted in Part II, will assist inexperienced associate lawyers in producing the useful work products that supervising attorneys expect and clients are willing to purchase. To meet this expectation, each assigned lawyer must meet another set of expectations that he or she will:

- understand and clarify assignments;
- manage workload, time, and assignments;
- communicate progress and the status of assignments; and
- develop meeting and telephone skills.

The text is supplemented by a series of forms and checklists that facilitate the application of these expectations to practice. Appendix A provides a "Client Service Checklist: Determining the Client's Needs and Expectations." Appendix B is a checklist to gauge "Communicating Effectively From the Client's Perspective." Appendix C is a "Client Service Audit: Corporate Counsel's Evaluation." And Appendices D through H are tools designed to aid new lawyers to better carry out their assignments: "Checklist of Assignment Ground Rules," "Case Flow Chart," "To Do List," "Assignment Management Worksheet," and "Worksheet for Meeting Preparation."

As you recognize and address these supervising attorney and client expectations, and some of the unstated underpinnings of effective law practice, you will be able to more rapidly define and refine your workstyle and approach to the delivery of client services in this increasingly competitive business and profession.

PART I

Expectations of Clients

1

Introduction to Part I

§ 1.01 GENERALLY

Law firms are businesses – as well as law practices – that sell professional services to existing and prospective clients. Attracting and maintaining clients requires practical understanding and sensitivity to clients' goals, priorities, and service expectations. When a lawyer considers a client's expectations unimportant, he or she may find that even excellent legal work becomes poor service that the client will refuse to purchase. Several client expectations affect the assignments of junior associates even though most client contact may be indirect. Therefore, Part I introduces client expectations of the lead or supervising attorney and team generally, within some contexts in which they arise.

A client may be unable to assess and rank the quality of legal work among technically competent lawyers.

That same client is, however, an excellent judge of whether he or she is pleased with a lawyer's "service." When a client perceives that technical competence is comparable among lawyers, that client selects the lawyer who makes it clear that he or she is interested in what the client wants to accomplish and will respond with superior professional judgment.

§ 1.02 NO ROOM FOR ASSUMPTIONS

Many lawyers frequently make tacit assumptions — consciously or unconsciously — about what clients want or "should want," the importance and relative priority that each client places on these goals, expected response time, and cost. Disasters often result when new lawyers make assumptions about a client's goal and priorities without valid supporting information. As one senior partner, a former naval officer, continually admonishes his firm's associates, "Never assume if you want to make admiral."

For many of you, disasters resulting from haphazard assumptions are within recent memory: recall that one instance — would that it were only one — where your brilliant substantive analysis, built on an unfounded factual assumption, was shelled by an unfeeling professor or, worse, by a smug fellow student in the next aisle. More than your unwarranted assumptions and ego stands to be shattered in the real world; you also jeopardize

- Your reputation as a thoughtful attorney,
- Your relationship with your supervising attorneys,
- Your firm's relationship with the client, and
- Your relationship with the firm.

§ 1.03 STUDY YOUR FIRM'S PHILOSOPHY, OBJECTIVES, AND EXPECTATIONS

When you receive an assignment on a new client matter, try to find out why the client selected an attorney in your firm. Develop a sense of how the firm and the originating attorney define and shape the firm's philosophy and distinguish it from its competitors. What kind of philosophy does the firm have and project? What "products" and services does it have and what are its markets? Examples of various approaches abound. Some firms are dedicated to client relationships and provide full service to their clients. Others specialize in sophisticated transactional business, provide "boutique" services, or serve particular industries. The character of a firm's representation also varies. Some firms assess risks more aggressively than others in the course of client representation.

By the time you have accepted a position with a firm, you ought to be in a pretty fair position to determine the firm's philosophy, major services and "products," and key client markets. In a perfect world, you and the interviewing attorneys would have discussed these points. If, as in most cases, this did not occur, you should spend time becoming familiar with the overall objectives, commitments, and expectations of your firm.

§ 1.04 OVERVIEW OF CLIENT EXPECTATIONS

What are the most common client expectations? How do the supervising attorney and firm team meet them? How do they affect your assignment?

Clients have certain legitimate expectations of their lawyers. The 20 expectations that follow reflect a distillation of those expectations most frequently expressed by clients and observed by their lawyers. While each client may not have all of these expectations, most are shared by clients to some degree. For example, all clients want their attorneys to understand what they want to accomplish and to be accessible (§§ 2.02, 3.03 [Part I, Expectations No. 1 and No. 8]), but not all clients need their attorneys to serve as a resource (§ 4.07 [Part I, Expectation No. 18]).

In addition, the emphasis of a single client's expectations may change from matter to matter. Therefore, a client-directed attorney monitors his or her client's expectations throughout the relationship, even as a single transaction evolves, is closed, and another begins.

Relate these 20 client expectations to your assignments. How do you identify and meet those that are important to a particular client?

Clients expect lawyers to:

1. Understand what the client wants to do.
2. Explain what is needed from the client.
3. Determine the role each lawyer will fill.
4. Estimate a timetable, fees, and costs.
5. Adjust unrealistic client expectations.
6. Determine special handling procedures.
7. Communicate progress and status.
8. Be accessible and return calls.
9. Respond promptly.
10. Ask for feedback.
11. Use the client's language.
12. Coordinate service.
13. Understand the client's business.
14. Consider the practical aspects.
15. Spot related problems.
16. Design responsive solutions.
17. Use economic sense.
18. Serve as a resource.
19. Update clients on new legal developments and techniques.
20. Understand the expectations of a corporate law department.

A client may express some of these expectations and may only imply others. The client may directly voice a concern about whether a lawyer is familiar enough with the client's industry; that same client may only imply that he or she expects the lawyer to "quarterback" the pieces of a project that other outside advisors will work on. An attorney may be able to anticipate some client expectations based upon prior dealings with that client. Originating and lead attorneys usually play the most important roles in determining, translating, and then communicating a client's overall expectations to other lawyers (and staff) assigned to that client's matter.

The following sections analyze each of the 20 expectations and provide a context for them. Become acquainted with these expectations as they affect a supervising attorney's demands on you. Your firm's style and attention to delivery of client service is a hallmark and marketing tool.

2

Over the Threshold: The Engagement

§ 2.01 EXPECTATIONS ONE THROUGH SIX

Clients expect lawyers to:

No. 1 Understand what the client wants to do.

No. 2 Explain what is needed from the client.

No. 3 Determine the role each lawyer will fill.

No. 4 Estimate a timetable, fees, and costs.

No. 5 Adjust unrealistic client expectations.

No. 6 Determine special handling procedures.

See Appendix A, Client Service Checklist: Determining the Client's Needs and Expectations.

§ 2.02 EXPECTATION NO. 1: UNDERSTAND WHAT THE CLIENT WANTS TO DO

Elementary, you say? Admittedly — yet this is exactly where the first, most haphazard, and most devastating assumption is most often made. A frequently heard client complaint is that the lawyer did not understand what needed to be done in the first place, "He never understood the problem! No wonder he could not hope to get me out of it." Coupled with this complaint is the oft-heard remark that: "My lawyer never even told me of that alternative. I only learned from Terry at a dinner party that I could. . . ." Both of these examples illustrate the danger of assumptions. Lawyers must ascertain what the client wants and establish the ground rules for the engagement. Some lawyers are so consumed by the desire to impress a new client with their achievements for others that they neglect to realize that the client wants to know what they can do for them — and *now*. These lawyers not only assume that they know what the client wants, but also fail to listen to the client's actual goal or problem. Their war stories are just cocktail talk, and they miss the opportunity to discuss their experience and expertise in the context of the client's problem.

You must determine where you are going before you begin: what does the *client* want to accomplish? Though you may not yet have direct client contact, it is imperative that you understand how your assignment fits into the supervising attorney's workplan to reach that client's goal. Experienced lawyers recognize that their clients value their judgment as well as their legal skills. Indeed, that judgment is a crucial resource to clients: it assists them in examining and clarifying the practical aspects of a goal that may dominate the legal issues. It also allows some clients to recognize and resolve problems that they have not otherwise seen. To tap this resource, however, you must know what the client wants to accomplish.

What the client *really* wants to accomplish is often not easily determined. The lawyer must pay close attention to how the client expresses his or her desires and needs. In some instances, the client will accurately identify problems. A lawyer will most often find this happy circumstance when dealing with the client's corporate law department attorneys, who are sophisticated consumers of your firm's legal services. *See* § 4.09 [Part I, Expectation No. 20: "Understand the Expectations of A Corporate Law Department"]. Nonlawyer clients, however, may not communicate precisely or neatly frame their objectives for the lawyer. Clients often do not separate or accurately label their thoughts. Instead, some clients may express a desired result, a strategy or means to achicve a result, a short or long range plan, or a combination of all of these. Others think aloud and express their thoughts as conclusions or directives, while still others use legal jargon incorrectly to state objectives. Some clients state what they believe will achieve the objective, while they remain completely unaware of other available means for achieving that goal. Two possible situations are likely if a lawyer is instantly ready to "gather the facts": the lawyer has either accepted what the client has said without analysis or has decided what the client *should* want instead of listening to what the client is saying.

Lawyers must also *ask questions* to figure out what clients want to accomplish. If clients say what they wanted or otherwise expresses a solution or action, but does not offer an objective, careful lawyers back up and determine exactly what that client really wants to do. They ask questions and restate the responses elicited to clarify the objective. These questions are tools used to refine the client's concerns, to clarify why the client has emphasized certain facts, and to determine whether what the client is saying is what is really meant: Is there more than one way to interpret what the client is saying? This process ensures that the lawyer will understand what the client means and will also prompt the client to elaborate upon, clarify, or rethink answers. Concerns, facts, and the overall goal are revealed in the process. When this is not done, formidable problems can occur.

CONSIDER:

The client, a computer entrepreneur, asked the company's regular outside lawyer to draft employment contracts for several executives. The client stated that a four-year contract with a "noncompete" provision was all that was necessary. The client did not offer any additional information except that the contracts should be ready for signing within a week. Before this conversation, the client had never mentioned the subject of employment contracts or expressed concerns about retaining key employees. The lawyer conducted a brief inquiry that focused only upon a few substantive issues in addition to dates, times, places, and names. Based on the client's responses to these questions, the lawyer prepared and timely sent the employment contracts to the client.

Actual result:

Each executive reacted to the noncompetition provisions with disbelief and refused to enter into the contract.

What went wrong?

Did the lawyer ever find out the client's concern or objective? Did the client give the lawyer any basis for understanding the problem that the client hoped to "solve"? No. The client simply had directed the lawyer to take an action the client thought would solve an undisclosed concern. The client's ambiguous and sketchy responses to the few questions asked should have alerted the lawyer to the potential prematurity of this "plan." The lawyer had inadequate information to assess whether an employment contract and noncompetition provision was an appropriate solution. To avoid this problem, the lawyer should have clarified the client's objective. Here, the lawyer did not understand the client's concern: that if its new, valuable technology were disclosed to competitors, the company would lose its competitive advantage. The client was seeking to protect the company's proprietary information and not to prevent an individual from joining a competitor. The technology had been developed by a consortium of outside consultants and it was unlikely that an individual executive could immediately hurt the company's business without this technology.

What should the lawyer have done?

What are some questions the lawyer could have asked to understand what the client really wanted to accomplish? Here are some suggestions.

- Why do you want employment contracts for executives who have already been on board for a couple of years?
- Are you happy with the performance of these executives?
- How valuable are they to the company?
- Are they loyal?
- Is morale good?
- Do you want to change the compensation arrangements?
- Have you discussed with them the possibility of employment contracts?

- Are you concerned that they will compete with you?
- What are your goals for the company over the next few years?

In this case, the client's responses would have prompted the lawyer to evaluate and discuss a nondisclosure agreement as a solution. Why didn't the client simply present the lawyer with the problem and ask the lawyer to suggest an appropriate solution? There are probably a variety of reasons. This client wanted every idea acted upon yesterday. By the time he called his lawyer, he was impatient for action and believed he knew what that action should be. The first solution that popped into his head was a legal buzz word, "noncompete," and a common legal housing for that provision was the employment contract. Perhaps colleagues on the golf course had mentioned the need for employment contracts in their companies and this client seized on their solution out of context and attached it to his problem. Probably this client would have been receptive to questions, but would not have thought to initiate a discussion to flesh out his objective.

Some clients may not be receptive to open ended questions, believing they already know what they want and only need legal assistance to draft documentation. In such a situation, the lawyer can begin with narrow questions to guide the client into recognizing that there are more decisions to be made first. For example, the lawyer might ask, "How did you handle. . . .?"

The point is that the lawyer should double check the client's solution. Remember, if the client becomes dissatisfied with his earlier solution, he will not hesitate to ask the lawyer why he did not tell him about alternatives; nor will the client hesitate to tell friends that the lawyer was not very good. The client will have to live with the legal effect and the lawyer may have to live without new business from the client or referrals. When the objective is understood by lawyer and client alike, however, the likelihood of a good outcome is increased.

CONSIDER:

A client calls and asks the partner to begin foreclosure proceedings against a tenant of a large warehouse the client owns. The partner delegates this assignment to an associate but first directs the associate to find out whether litigation is the best solution for the client.

What went right?

The client expressed a request in terms of a solution, rather than presenting the partner with the problem. The associate knows that the tenant has occupied the premises for at least two years because the associate had previously drafted the lease agreement for the warehouse. To determine whether litigation is the best solution, what questions would you ask the client?

Here the associate covered the following:

- Whether the leasing arrangement with the tenant has been satisfactory over the past two years.
- How many payments the tenant has missed.
- How many late payments the tenant has made.
- What has caused the tenant's financial problems and the extent to which they are being resolved.
- How easy it would be to get another tenant.

The associate learned that the tenant recently suffered some financial problems because of overestimating inventory for the summer season. Although the tenant has tried to come current on lease payments, the tenant is still two months behind. Before this inventory problem, the client had paid promptly. The tenant has maintained the property in excellent repair. Warehouse vacancies in the area are high and the client is concerned about having cash flow difficulties from meeting debt service on the property during the period it would probably be vacant until another suitable tenant is located. Before encountering difficulties, the tenant had indicated a desire to exercise an option to renew the lease and to negotiate a second option; the client had been willing to enter into such an arrangement.

What alternatives would you encourage the client to explore before deciding what to do?

Here, by refraining from blindly obeying the client's original directive, the attorney discovered the client's unstated concern — cash flow and a new lease agreement — and objective — protecting his immediate interests. The associate absorbed this information and said, "From what you've just told me, it appears you are really concerned with securing a steady stream of income from the property to cover your debt service. Do you really want to get rid of this tenant if we can arrange a workout?" By asking questions first, the associate was able to guide the client to focus on the real objective — securing an uninterrupted cash flow from the property — and then to consider an alternative solution to protect his immediate interests. The associate and client arranged for the tenant to pay a reduced rent that would cover the client's debt service, to escalate rent in the tenant's option year, and to renegotiate the option.

APPLYING THIS EXPECTATION TO YOUR RESPONSIBILITIES

Find out how your assignment fits into the supervising attorney's strategy to accomplish the client's objective.

Ask yourself:

How does my assignment fit into the client's overall objective?

Do I understand the client's definition of a "win?"

What are the client's priorities and concerns?

Do I know the supervising attorney's strategy as it affects my assignment?

---

§ 2.03 EXPECTATION NO. 2: EXPLAIN WHAT YOU NEED FROM THE CLIENT

While a client has a duty to cooperate, it is up to the lawyer to inform that client in a timely manner of what is needed and expected. For example, to save time in analyzing a tax litigation case, the lawyer might ask the client to organize receipts, records, and other written material by certain classifications. Some other outside advisors do this routinely. In working with a new client, CPAs educate the client on record-keeping as a matter of course, to make their staff's efforts more efficient. When requesting such information or documents, explain why it is necessary or helpful, if its relevance is not readily apparent to the client. Give the client deadlines to avoid any misunderstanding on when the requested information is needed and expected. Also consider presenting clients with the option of obtaining data that lawyers and staff could gather less cost-effectively than the client. Send a letter confirming what the client has been requested (and has committed) to do and when you expect the task to be completed. Depending on the circumstances and the time frame, you may also want to calendar a date by which you should follow up on the client's progress.

Sometimes lawyers advise clients to wait until the lawyers have taken an action or checked on something before going ahead with a plan. Some lawyers, however, will instruct a client cryptically, "Don't do anything until you hear from me." Such a directive, if not coupled with an estimate of when the client will hear from the counsellor, is often impractical from the client's perspective. The client's business continues and the client may have to make decisions that affect, or will be affected by, the situation the lawyer is handling. This type of directive also has the effect of excluding the client from the process; the lawyer may have lost sight of who is the principal and who is the agent. Clients expect at least an estimate of when they will hear from the lawyer and — absent an explanation of what the client can do, should not do and why — the client may ignore the instruction. These negative directives are confusing, uninformative, and provide no basis from which the client can judge whether an action taken during the interim will be innocuous or harmful.

APPLYING THIS EXPECTATION TO YOUR RESPONSIBILITIES

Determine and communicate clearly to the supervising attorney, or client (if appropriate):

What you need from the client or other source.

Why you need it.

When you need it.

Calendar your follow-up date.

Follow up on progress, receipt.

---

§ 2.04 EXPECTATION NO. 3: DETERMINE THE ROLE EACH LAWYER WILL FILL

Clients often have definite ideas about the role they want their lawyers to play in an engagement. Therefore, the lead attorney must discuss and determine the role(s) and style that counsel are to assume. The roles vary from case to case and may even change during the course of a single transaction or case. How the lead attorney determines the team's roles and style is similar to how he or she figures out the client's objective. Knowledge of the client's business and operating style, gained from either the client or members of the firm, is crucial to accurately assessing that client's expectation of the lawyers' role.

One thing is certain: the client does not expect the lawyers to be disinterested referees in the process. In addition to giving legal advice, supervising attorneys and associates often play the following roles:

Sounding Board
Quarterback
Coordinator
Educator
Stress Manager
Litigator
General Counsel

The originating or responsible attorney may also serve the client in the capacity of a "liaison partner."

§ 2.04(a) Sounding Board

A client may call upon a lawyer to brainstorm, analyze, and investigate ideas that are still in an early stage. *See* § 4.07 [Part I, Expectation No. 18: "Serve as a Resource"]. For example, a large grocery chain makes the services of a trauma team available to its store employees who were in the store during a robbery and murder. Management is considering extension of this service to customers who were also present. The executive vice president decides to brainstorm with counsel before looking into the idea further. Counsel investigates how some other corporations faced with similar situations have handled them and then discusses pros and cons and potential liability issues and damages exposure with the client.

§ 2.04(b) Quarterback

Occasionally, clients present a situation and expect it to be handled with a minimum of their own involvement. The client expects the lawyer to understand the objective, figure out an appropriate course of action, map out a strategy to reach that objective, and obtain the result. The lawyer must be careful to read this expectation correctly because other clients expect to be involved in some or all of the above steps and will be dissatisfied if the lawyer presumes this to be his or her role exclusively. *See,* for example, § 4.09 [Part I, Expectation No. 20: "Understand Expectations of A Corporate Law Department"].

§ 2.04(c) Coordinator

Attorneys may be expected to guide and coordinate client participation and actions. In litigation, attorneys coordinate as well as direct clients' activities surrounding discovery requests. This role, of course, is not limited to coordination in layman's terms. The lawyer does not say to the client, "Give me everything you have on this particular issue that is relevant." The lawyer asks for files and determines what is relevant. In instructing the client to answer interrogatories, the lawyer does not merely transmit the other side's interrogatories without instructions in a cover letter. Instead, the lawyer's instructions, depending on the situation, may go something like, "I need you to sketch out answers to interrogatories 6 through 10, 16, 18, and 22; please send your answers to us by. . . ." Or, "I will call in the next five days for your answers. Then I will incorporate your answers and send your responses to the interrogatories to you for review." This role often is conducted in tandem with the role of educator. It is up to the lawyers not only to inform the client of their expectations but also to clarify or explain them in a timely manner. In this example, the lawyer would explain to the client that the answers to these interrogatories are required by law and that the lawyer already has the information to draft answers to those interrogatories that are not listed.

On the business or transactional side of the practice, an attorney must often coordinate various activities of third parties as well as those within the firm to complete and formalize a business deal, even though certain responsibilities for negotiation rest with the client and other advisors. For example, in a complex combination of several existing partnerships coordination involves accounting, valuation, engineering, and economic analyses that must be integrated and made a part of the contract for the client to close the deal on time. Obviously, an attorney's function here extends beyond pure legal advice.

§ 2.04(d) Educator

A lawyer's role as educator includes two aspects. First, lawyers can assist the client in understanding the ramifications of alternatives and recommended action. In this role, the lawyer enables a client to make a more informed decision. The role of "assault team member" (*see* "Litigator" below) sometimes evolves into that of an educator. The attorney may decide that there are more effective approaches for attaining the client's ultimate goal and, therefore, undertakes to educate the client to consider these alternatives to reach the result.

Second, an attorney can prepare the client to handle the same or similar circumstances in the future by making the client familiar and comfortable with the legal aspects of recurring situations. For example, you can prepare or review standard forms, or train an employee to handle anticipated events such as documenting routine corporate actions. You may also use newsletters or an in-house seminar to update a client on procedures that need to be changed because of new laws or agency regulations.

In most instances, a client appreciates the education and the opportunity to become self-sufficient to handle recurring situations without calling the lawyer each time. Acting in the role of educator can be a process for weaning the client from dependence upon the attorney. This approach, however, often generates increased respect for the attorney's expertise and economic sense and can prompt the client to use the attorney more often in developing plans and procedures.

§ 2.04(e) Stress Manager

Do not misunderstand this role as "the lawyer as nanny." Admittedly, a client may choose an attorney partly to eliminate stress and to manage potentially troublesome pressures on the client's own time, resources, or patience. In the litigation process, attorneys "take the heat" from opposing counsel, and, in fact, deflect the more unpleasant aspects of litigation from the client (onto the attorney). A client may want the attorney to reinforce its positions in unpopular situations or transactions. For example, when the employee relations department of a company is dissatisfied with house counsel's opinion that sets forth certain steps that should be taken before terminating an employee, the company's law department engages outside counsel to give a presentation to the employee relations department that reinforces the law department's advice.

§ 2.04(f) Litigator

A lawyer's role as litigator can take on a range of tones and approaches, depending on what the client wants: What is a "win" to that client? Litigation often affects other areas of a client's business and cannot be viewed as an isolated occurrence. Priorities in exploring alternative dispute resolution or in pursuing litigation vary among clients and as a case progresses. For example, a client may want to settle quickly to remove the specter of contingent liability before undertaking a transaction. Or, the client may want to resume or continue a relationship with the other side but teach a lesson at the same time. The latter situation would dictate a restrained tone; a different approach would be required if the client insisted that its adversary's case was without merit. Clarifying the role, in turn, lays the groundwork for assessing strategy in managing the litigation: what should and should not be done.

Frequently the firm team is called upon to be a member of "the A team." Its function as a member of the client's "assault team" is often to act as an enforcer or a "hired gun." When lawyers are placed in this role, the client expects aggressive representation because he or she is firmly committed to litigation. Clients often articulate such a plan of action with a variation of "I want you to fight this," or "I want this guy off my back.

I'm tired of being pushed around, so let's fight back." Be alert, however, to any change in the client's attitude toward an adversary. A client's situation is fluid, not static. Some time after a client has directed that a pleading be filed, the intensity of emotion may have lessened. Or, a business opportunity may have arisen — with the adversary! As the supervising attorney makes adjustments in tone and strategy, do not be surprised if you are instructed to adjust your style or tactics accordingly.

Sometimes the supervising attorney may determine that the client's objective is inappropriate. A client may have an unrealistic or naive view of the probability of a "win" in light of the case's lack of merit or he may misunderstand the lawyer's function. The lawyer may be faced with a situation requiring delicate handling: let the client blow off steam until he or she is ready to deal with the facts and the cost of company time. The lawyers may need to immediately expand their roles to include the functions of educator-counselors to explain why the particular suit appears to be a good candidate for early resolution, while they continue to represent the client aggressively. One client recently remarked of his lawyer, "Our lawyer is outstanding; he tells us when it is more cost-effective not to pursue a legalistic solution." It is also essential to keep the client advised of progress and status so that the client may reassess objectives and strategy at regular intervals. Of course, if the lawyer determines through reasonable inquiry that a client's claim or defense is frivolous, the lawyer would be subject to sanctions were he or she to proceed. *See* Fed. R. Civ. P. 11.

CONSIDER:

In a custody modification action, the client proposes joint custody to the former spouse. Initially, the spouse appears receptive. A week later, the client abruptly informs the lawyer that joint custody is not really important; he wants to go to court to "run her through the mill." The lawyer explains that the purpose of the modification statute is to protect the best interest of the child. The lawyer refuses to pursue the action simply for the client to gouge the custodial parent. The lawyer withdraws.

§ 2.04(g) General Counsel

Often a client, without a developed legal department, wants an attorney to monitor the client's ongoing operations and advise it about the legal aspects. This may include fielding questions or complaints or providing legal guidance in everyday matters. In general, clients also expect attorneys to keep abreast of current legal developments and advise them of matters that affect them personally or professionally. Accessibility is a primary expectation of a client who wants this type of service. *See* § 3.03 [Part I, Expectation No. 8: "Be Accessible and Return Calls"].

§ 2.04(h) Liaison Partner

Some clients expect the attorney who originated the

business to remain in touch with the progress of a matter even if another lawyer is handling the day-to-day work or is the lead attorney and formulates overall strategy. This liaison role provides the client with an emergency lever to correct any problem that the client would be uncomfortable discussing with the lawyer actually handling the matter. To fill this role effectively, a liaison partner must be accessible and have the power internally to facilitate changes in personnel or in strategy as needed to maintain client satisfaction. The originating partner must also stay in touch with the lawyers who are handling the client's work. Accounting firms commonly assign an account manager whose responsibility is to stay in touch with a client. The liaison partner is also well positioned to recognize and respond to opportunities to cross-sell the firm's services.

APPLYING THIS EXPECTATION TO YOUR RESPONSIBILITIES

Understand for each matter:

The supervising attorney's role and responsibilities.

Your role
Your responsibilities
Your authority
Your accountability

The client's (and staff's) role and responsibilities.

---

§ 2.05 EXPECTATION NO. 4: ESTIMATE A TIMETABLE, FEES, AND COSTS

Most clients want to know how long their legal work will take and how much it will cost. The days of proclaiming, "I'll do them a good job at a fair price" no longer exist. Sophisticated clients and those with legal departments expect lawyers to estimate the time and cost required to reach the objective or solve the problem. Increasingly, corporate clients and outside counsel spend time at the outset to reduce estimates to budgets that project partner, associate, and legal assistant rates and the time needed to produce the most cost-effective allocation.

§ 2.05(a) Time Estimates

Clients usually have a belief, an expectation, or a requirement for the amount of time in which the legal services should be performed and the objective reached. Absent a discussion about how long an assignment or a matter will take to complete, the client and lawyer may hold vastly different perceptions.

The lawyer's understanding of the client's objectives, motivation, priorities, and other plans that are affected by the matter, is critical in structuring a workable timetable and action plan. When communicating a time estimate, the lawyer should realize that a client may rely upon it. The lawyer can also assume that the client may become dissatisfied with the lawyer's service if dates are missed without explanation, even though the legal work was of high quality. A lawyer is well advised to educate the client about the components of a timeline that are dictated by technical legal requirements or that may change if certain complications occur. Then, if a problem arises, the lawyer can refer back to those earlier discussions and explain the revision to the estimate. Without communication about the process, a client may be surprised to learn that "delays" have occurred and assign blame to the lawyer. For example, when making a settlement offer to a government agency, consider that its normal processing time may be substantially greater than that encountered with another private party. Explain that to the client.

CONSIDER:

The client informs the lawyer that he needs an answer by the middle of the day. Based upon factors he outlines, the client asks the lawyer whether there is an unacceptable risk in his plan to acquire a business.

The lawyer conducts research, confers with another lawyer, and advises the client against the acquisition if the client's only alternatives are to undertake it immediately or to forego it. He explains the risk that the client would inherit two liabilities upon acquisition of the company, and advises that this legal risk is too high based on the limited information the client possesses. He continues his assessment by saying that there might be a way to reduce the risk or the liabilities to an acceptable level if a few more days were available.

The lawyer outlines the strategy to gather necessary information to structure negotiations to reduce the risk, and a timetable for the next week to implement the strategy. With this understanding of the risk, the lawyer's strategy, and the timetable, the client reconsiders his timing objective and concludes that the acquisition would still make sense if delayed a week.

§ 2.05(b) Fees and Costs

Many clients want the lawyer to initiate a discussion of how much their legal services will cost and they want a better idea of price than a range of hourly rates. Clients increasingly expect lawyers to estimate fees and expenses. Some clients assume that a fee estimate represents a maximum amount unless the lawyer clearly indicates otherwise.

In monitoring the work performed on a matter, the lawyer may anticipate that an estimate will be exceeded. If so, prompt communication allows the lawyer and client to reassess the course of action. Conversely, the lawyer's failure to prepare the client for a bill that exceeds the estimate results in a client who is surprised and dissatisfied even though the services were reasonable and appropriate.

A fee agreement or engagement letter defines the initial expectations of the client and serves as the basis for the attorney's work. It is usually the first written communication between the attorney and client. Ideally it addresses the lawyer's understanding of the client's objective, the scope (and limits) of representation and work that the lawyer is committed to perform, and includes a fee arrangement. The fee letter should cover items the client wants to know and discuss, such as the billing schedule, a laundry list of expenses for which the client will be charged (and may have otherwise assumed were part of the firm's overhead) and how they will be handled, who else may work on the matter, their rates, the average rate, or the blended rate (if the matter is priced on the basis of hourly rates rather than billed at a fixed price). If the client has agreed to assume certain responsibilities, it may be appropriate to include them in the agreement. If, however, the agreement is vague on a point or "ground rule," the client or attorney may later cite it in support of an assumption or intention.

CONSIDER:

• A new client is forming a mortgage company. He and his partner want to budget attorneys' fees into their *pro forma* for the start up expenses in their business plan. They ask for an estimate of fees to expect for advice on "routine" questions that will come up during the creation and early months of operation, as separate from the fees for preparation of the documents and filings.

• A client asks for a fee estimate for drafting private placement offering documents and the formation of a limited partnership. The securities lawyer prepares an estimate after conferring with the tax department to obtain their cost estimate for a tax opinion based on the lawyer's understanding of the deal. The lawyer advises that, if the client changes the deal, the fee may change to reflect the new factors.

APPLYING THIS EXPECTATION TO YOUR RESPONSIBILITIES

Adhere to deadlines.

Estimate carefully timetables you are asked to prepare. The client and supervising attorney will rely on them.

Anticipate and promptly communicate to the supervising attorney proposed changes in your estimated timetable or increases in hours needed to complete your assignment.

Develop a sense of the range of fees and expenses for types of matters in which you are involved.

---

§ 2.06 EXPECTATION NO. 5: ADJUST UNREALISTIC CLIENT EXPECTATIONS

The process of listening to and then questioning a client also assists the lawyer in discovering any unrealistic expectations the client may have about the lawyer's role and responsibilities or his power to achieve an objective. The client may believe, for example, that the lawyer can "make the IRS go away." Or, in a litigation context (*see* § 2.04(f) [Part I, Expectation No. 3: "Determine the Role Each Lawyer Will Fill" under "Litigator"]), a client may believe that as soon as he engages a lawyer or "dumps the problem onto the lawyer's lap," he can relax; the case becomes the lawyer's problem. It is up to the lawyer to educate that type of client about his or her continuing involvement in the case. It may be important for the lawyer to discuss the relative costs that will be incurred if the lawyer performs "footwork" that the client could as readily do.

A client often arrives at the lawyer's office believing that the case is airtight; an outcome of less than total victory is unthinkable. If the final result does not meet that expectation, the client will be frustrated and irritated with or disappointed in the lawyer. The lawyer must be alert to recognize a client's potentially unrealistic beliefs and educate the client about various factors that may work against his position. Similarly, the lawyer must guard against creating an unrealistic expectation by giving the client an overly optimistic assessment of the case. If the lawyer's prediction proves to be wrong, it could result in a call to the grievance committee or damaging grumbling on the street.

A client's unrealistic expectations may stem from a lack of familiarity with litigation rules or processes. A client company involved in litigation in an unfamiliar jurisdiction may erroneously assume that certain favorable rules apply or that the case will come to trial within a short period of time. For example, a client may request that his lawyer file a suit immediately. The lawyer may determine that there is no immediate statute of limitations pressure that precludes reasonable inquiry into the merit of the claim before filing. It is the lawyer's role to explain to the client why the lawyer has an ethical obligation to investigate a key witness before he will draft and file a complaint. *See* Fed. R. Civ. P. 11.

For another example, a client believes that the lawyer will recommend an appropriate insurance product to fund a buy-sell agreement that he and his partners want to create. This is an unrealistic expectation of what the lawyer is going to do in a planning context. The lawyer can, however, correct this misunderstanding by telling the client that she will suggest some insurance brokers for the client to contact to locate a competitive product for this need and then will review the proposals and illustrations prepared by those brokers.

A client may also have an unrealistic expectation of his or her regular lawyer when the client is acting in a capacity other than that of client. Suppose a real estate broker, who is also a regular client, is working with a seller. The broker wants to "send" the seller over to the lawyer's office to "get a letter to put in the file that says. . . ." The lawyer cannot permit the broker to direct his or her professional judgment in rendering an opinion. The lawyer, therefore, makes that clear to the broker. Then if the broker decides to recommend that the seller go to that lawyer, the lawyer can make an independent business decision as to whether to render legal services to the seller. *See* Model Rules of Professional Conduct, Rules 2.3 and 5.4 (Proposed Final Draft 1981).

APPLYING THIS EXPECTATION TO YOUR RESPONSIBILITIES

Report to the supervising attorney any unrealistic expectations or misunderstandings you find that a client has about:

Responsibilities

Assessment of probable result

Cost

Timetable

Process

---

§ 2.07 EXPECTATION NO. 6: DETERMINE SPECIAL HANDLING PROCEDURES

Special handling procedures or instructions frequently govern areas such as communication channels, correspondence, billing format and detail, reimburseable expenses, review, format for written reports, use of client staff, and so forth. During the engagement process the lead lawyer should find out from and discuss with the client any expectations as to procedural rules to be followed by the firm members in performing that client's legal work. Some clients with law departments have formulated detailed written procedures that create a framework or structure for the relationship. Occasionally a client wants some procedures that may be unworkable. By discussing what the client wants or needs, the lawyer and the client can begin to design workable solutions to fulfill those needs.

CONSIDER:

A client company specifies that outside counsel is expected to provide 60 days notice of trial settings. The local court rules in the jurisdiction governing the case, however, give only 30 days notice. After explaining the local rule, the outside lawyer and the client work out another reporting arrangement that satisfies the client's concern that trial strategy and negotiating positions be reviewed and managed properly.

A lawyer who is unfamiliar with the client's operations may find certain procedures unimportant or arbitrary. Be assured, however, that they are important to the client and, if disregarded, will become a source of great irritation.

CONSIDER:

Several weeks before the next statement for professional services was due, the client's chief financial officer mentioned to an attorney who was not the billing partner that he wanted only a composite entry to appear on the bill for preparation of a work product. He explained that it was too time consuming for the department to sort and process large numbers of entries relating to preparation of a group of documents. Upon receiving and reviewing the statement a few weeks later, he was annoyed to see separate entries for successive drafts of documentation. He telephoned the billing partner to complain and learned that his request was news to the partner.

**APPLYING THIS EXPECTATION
TO YOUR RESPONSIBILITIES**

Find out whether any special handling procedures govern your:

Communication channels

Correspondence

Time reporting increments, descriptions

Expenses

Status Reports

Appendix A is a worksheet on which to record engagement data that is relevant to your project. Find out what relevant data is recorded on the firm's new matter intake form.

3

Ongoing Communication: Demonstrating the Value of Service

---

§ 3.01 EXPECTATIONS SEVEN THROUGH TWELVE

Clients expect lawyers to:

No. 7 Communicate progress and status.

No. 8 Be accessible and return calls.

No. 9 Respond promptly.

No. 10 Ask for feedback.

No. 11 Use the client's language.

No. 12 Coordinate service.

§ 3.02 EXPECTATION NO. 7: COMMUNICATE PROGRESS AND STATUS

It is axiomatic that your clients do not know or understand what you are doing for them unless you regularly and clearly communicate your efforts and progress. Similarly, it is likely that your supervising attorneys do not know how you are progressing on a lengthy assignment unless you tell them. *See* § 6.05 [Part II, Expectation No. 6: "Communicate Progress and Status"]. Whatever the lawyer's role, part of your job is to communicate what you are doing and what you plan to do to achieve the objective the client seeks.

Lawyers must be alert to inform their clients of not only what they determine the client "needs to know," but also what the client has asked to know or has an interest in. The manner and frequency with which a client expects to be kept informed varies from client to client and from matter to matter. The engagement process and engagement letter should guide the lawyer in communicating effectively with the client. A client's expectations turn on the relative importance he or she attaches to a matter and that client's operating style. Some clients want a sense of control over what is going on and expect to be called frequently and to receive all correspondence. Some expect the lawyer to contact them only when a business decision needs to be made or an important development occurs, and prefer to receive most periodic reports in writing. As one client said, "You're not my broker or my tax advisor — only call me if it's urgent."

In all events, the lawyer should copy the client on correspondence that enters and leaves the office, with few exceptions. (An example of an exception is a corporate general counsel who instructs the outside lawyers to only send summaries to permit efficient management of a volume of matters. *See* § 4.09 [Part I, Expectation No. 20: "Understand the Expectations of a Corporate Law Department"]. Similarly, let the client know why nothing is happening when that is the case. For example, "I have not heard from the other side. It's to our advantage to sit tight right now because. . . ."

By providing the client with periodic reports, oral or written, and copies of correspondence, you:

- Demonstrate to the client that you are on top of their case.
- Provide a check to ensure you are following instructions the client gave or intended to give.
- Update the client on new developments and provide an opportunity to discuss options and reach decisions.
- Prepare the client to expect the statements for professional services.

Until a lawyer knows how frequently a particular client expects to be advised about work progress, more communication is better than less — but it is wise to ask. The attorney may determine what "regular and clear communication" means to a client by discovering how the client's business operates and how other advisors and employees report. Often, simple attention to the client's actions will also provide an indication of the frequency of communication the client expects. If, for example, a client telephones often about the status of a matter, the client may not feel sufficiently informed of progress and future steps. Not surprisingly, some clients are unhappy to learn that motions have been filed on their behalf weeks earlier. It is advisable that the lawyer follow up important oral communications with a letter summarizing the information, presenting an analysis of the alternatives, and confirming an understanding or decision reached. Discussing the matter regularly with the client, simultaneously copying the client on correspondence and memos, and submitting status reports all prepare the client to expect a bill that conforms to billing procedures agreed upon in the engagement letter, that describes services the client can relate back to the correspondence and discussions, and that is sent monthly unless otherwise agreed.

CONSIDER:

A corporate client desires to offer a new service to its field force. The company's senior vice president of marketing engages an outside law firm to analyze licensing requirements for various levels of service in the states within the company's marketing area. The originating attorney tells the vice president he estimates the project will require one month to complete. Because of unexpected complexities and delays in communicating with state authorities, the firm does not complete and mail the report until the end of the second month. Neither the originating attorney nor the team of firm members working on the project initiates progress reports during this two-month period. The vice president calls the firm after the first month and does not receive sufficient direction to allow him to answer questions about the delay from the impatient field force. He is also unable to provide a firm implementation date for the new service.

The completed report — a tome — does not begin with or contain a deductively-structured summary. Instead, the authors assumed the readers possessed substantial knowledge of the problem and understood how to implement the firm's recommendations!

To plan and carry out a practical course of action, the vice president had to initiate several conference calls among the originating attorney and the other attorneys who conducted the research and produced this report. The vice president did not appreciate the firm's effort or delayed results.

What went wrong?

As soon as the attorneys recognized that completion would be delayed, the originating attorney should have contacted the vice president for authorization to continue on that course, or for guidance on giving priority to some parts of the project over others. When the authors sat down to draft their report, they should have considered their audience: what format for the recommendations and procedures is easiest for the client to understand, what language is used by the client, and what time constraints does the client face in reading the report and in making decisions based upon its content?

In discussing a planned course of action, the lawyer should let the client know what to expect. Procedures that are routine to the lawyer may confuse the client, absent explanation. Without such assistance, the client may draw negative conclusions about the lawyer's interest, efforts, or skill. For example, suppose a litigation matter has claimed a substantial amount of a lawyer's attention and the client has received a steady stream of correspondence. Upon filing the pretrial order, the judge sets the trial for eight months later. The client should be told why the activity level will decrease for a few months. Effective communication requires the lawyer to be sensitive to the client's perceptions, to confer with and educate the client about the purpose of the process and the potential benefits, and to respond to the client's concerns.

CONSIDER:

Plaintiff sues your firm's client individually for allegedly misrepresenting some financial statements in a Regulation D offering. Seeking to pin down the claimed misrepresentations, you serve interrogatories and a request for production of documents. Plaintiff's counsel, whom you have met previously in pretrial preparation and who has behaved reasonably on procedural matters, requests an extension of time to respond because the plaintiff has been out of town for two weeks. You know that the client becomes enraged when the plaintiff's name is mentioned, and would undoubtedly view a request for the time of day as unreasonable. This client may well consider an extension a material and undesirable change in the timetable, even if that extension will not affect the trial date because the docket is backlogged and a trial date has not been set. You reflect on your definition of professional courtesy and decide that you will simply tell the client and the supervising attorney of your decision to agree to an extension.

What went wrong?

You expect the client to accept your assessment — as the supervising attorney and the firm have been hired specifically for their judgment in handling litigation matters, and for their professional abilities. Nevertheless, controlling the client does not mean ignoring or overriding the client's concerns. Before agreeing to an extension, you also want to be sensitive to the client's perspective and to assure the client that you have not given away the farm. Therefore, you must take the time to educate the client about the process and to reduce the level of anxiety. Explain how granting the request for extension can help the client later. Remember that many people, including otherwise sophisticated individuals, do not understand how lawyers can fight tooth and nail in or out of court and then amicably discuss procedural issues, converse socially, go out to lunch, or — if television can be believed — join in even more intimate exchanges.

The following considerations will help you evaluate your communication efforts, whether you report your progress and the status of an assignment to the supervising attorney or directly to the client. Ask yourself whether you have given the supervising attorney or client sufficient timely information for the client to:

- Follow progress.
- Ask questions intelligently.
- Develop and maintain confidence and trust in your judgment.
- Give feedback.
- Participate in strategic decision making.
- Carry out his or her responsibilities.
- Understand the use of outside resources.
- Decide on other plans affected.
- Deal effectively with the media.
- Relate billed effort to value received.
- Understand reasons for and discuss any material change in the timetable, cost, or strategy.

- Understand the qualifications, role, and efforts of each lawyer and legal assistant involved.

See Appendix B, Communicating Effectively from the Client's Perspective. It contains a checklist to test whether you have given sufficient timely information to the supervising attorney about the progress and status of your projects.

APPLYING THIS EXPECTATION TO YOUR RESPONSIBILITIES

Supervising attorneys must keep their clients informed.

To assist them:

Evaluate your communication efforts. Have you given sufficient, timely information?

Remember that a satisfied client can answer this question: "What is my lawyer doing for me?"

---

§ 3.03 EXPECTATION NO. 8: BE ACCESSIBLE AND RETURN CALLS

A client who is worried that the lawyer will be or is insufficiently accessible often voices this concern by saying something like, "Do you have time to handle my situation?" Accessibility is in large part demonstrated to a client by the prompt return of telephone calls and by proper handling of calls when the attorney is unavailable. Prompt return of telephone calls gives the client early assurance that the matter is important to the lawyer and the firm, has priority, and is receiving thoughtful and expeditious attention. Many lawyers are deservedly criticized by former and existing clients for failing to return nonurgent phone calls within a reasonable period of time — 24 hours. The reasons given for failure to return phone calls or otherwise remain accessible to the client are limited only by the creativity of the lawyer and staff:

The attorney was in trial.

The attorney was at a hearing.

The attorney was preparing for trial.

The attorney was in the library.

The attorney was preparing for/attending/conducting depositions.

The attorney stepped away from his or her desk.

The attorney had left for the day.

The attorney was out of the office for several days.

The attorney was on vacation.

The attorney was seeking clarification on the client's matter from another firm member and had not yet received it.

The attorney was waiting for the project to be completed by support staff.

The attorney was involved in an emergency "deal"/"transaction"/"emergency problem" and was unable to break free to return calls.

The attorney had attempted to call the client back but was unsuccessful.

The attorney did return the client's call but the client's secretary must not have delivered the message.

The attorney did not receive the client's messages.

The attorney was waiting for the client's secretary to call the attorney's secretary.

The attorney was on another line.

The computer was down.

A lawyer's *unstated* but obvious reasons for failing to return calls or to be accessible to the client include:

The attorney does not like the client.

The attorney does not like the project that the client has assigned.

The attorney is unsure of what advice to give the client.

The attorney has procrastinated in preparing whatever the client is expecting and, therefore, is loath to admit lack of action.

The attorney has made an unrealistic promise that an item would be ready and does not want to indicate to the expectant client that it was not completed or has not been started.

The attorney has not informed the secretary or other team members where he or she has gone.

The attorney has delegated the matter and does not know its status.

The attorney is rude.

The attorney is playing golf.

In many of these situations, the attorney is also making an assumption about what the call concerns — it could be an emergency, a new matter, or a referral!

Here are some suggestions to improve your accessibility:

• Develop an effective internal system with your secretary to maintain the caller's confidence that they have your ear through your secretary. Does your secretary know your schedule so that callers can be told when to expect you to return the call? Notify your secretary of incoming calls that you anticipate and give instructions for a message to the caller. Inform your secretary when you leave the office and estimate how long you expect to be out of the office. Let your secretary know where you can be reached.

• If you are going out of town, leave your secretary instructions to call those persons whom you want to inform of your absence and your return date or report status. For example, "Judy asked me to tell you she'll be back Thursday." Or ask your secretary to tell Mr. Brown that ". . . the contract has been signed and Miss Jones has talked with Mr. Brooks. We are proceeding on schedule as we discussed." If a legal assistant is working with you on the matter and has had contact with the client, in limited situations you may wish to instruct your secretary to ask whether the client would like to speak with the legal assistant in your absence.

• Have your secretary check off each message you receive each time you call into the office. A useful procedure is for your secretary to keep your telephone messages and notes from firm members on a sheet of paper or on a computer in the form of electronic mail instead of on individual slips. By reading over the sheet you will be brought up to date on what has happened in your absence.

• Place unreturned calls at the top of your *"To Do List."* For a discussion of the use of the *To Do List, see* § 6.03 [Part II, Expectation No. 4: "Manage Your Assignments"] Clients or outside advisors should never have the feeling that their calls, alone, prompted you to work on their problems or projects. If the client has expected a response, a call from you, or a status report, the client may believe that your silence means you are not managing the matter. In this situation, if you do not have information or answers to report when the client calls, the client may conclude that the telephone call is your "late warning system" to spur you into action to handle the matter.

• If you try to return a call but cannot reach the caller, consider asking his or her secretary when it would be convenient to call again or *set a telephone appointment.* Conversely, you should ensure that your client is accessible by obtaining emergency telephone numbers, as appropriate.

APPLYING THIS EXPECTATION TO YOUR RESPONSIBILITIES

Set up an accessibility system:

Inform your secretary of your whereabouts.

Anticipate calls; brief your secretary with appropriate messages and instructions.

Return nonemergency calls within 24 hours; arrange telephone appointments.

§ 3.04 EXPECTATION NO. 9: RESPOND PROMPTLY

Although lawyers may seem to be perfectionists by nature, few lawyers can afford the luxury of pursuing perfection. Indeed, in many assignments, supervising attorneys and clients do not expect every stone to be turned, and those clients are unwilling to incur the cost of delay or additional fees for exhaustive scrutiny. Clients do want a prompt response, want to know they are being actively represented, and want to be kept informed.

A client expects that its lawyers will devote attention to each of its matters within the time frame that the *client* perceives it should be handled, unless otherwise discussed. Lawyers often set or agree to unrealistic deadlines, setting themselves up for missed dates and setting their clients up for frustration. Frequently, a client does not have a specific deadline in mind, but thinks in terms of an acceptable range. If any deadline is offered, however, that client may seize upon it and elevate it to gospel status. If the client does not specifically ask for a deadline, the lawyer should refrain from offering any definite dates; instead, it is better to give the client a range of time to allow for flexibility in dealing with unforeseen problems. If a client requests a definite deadline, the lawyer should carefully assess available resources and the matter's requirements before making any promises.

Once established, *meet all deadlines* – whether imposed by the supervising attorney or by the client. If you find that it becomes impossible to comply with a deadline, however, inform the supervising attorney of the problem when it arises – *before* the assigned due date. Then the supervising attorney can evaluate whether to alter the course of action, confer with the client, and so forth.

CONSIDER:

A law firm delegated some of a client bank's real estate matters to a second year associate. The associate prepared the documents in draft and forwarded them to the bank for review. The bank executive expected the associate to complete the documents upon receipt of the bank's comments on the drafts. The banker then confirmed with the seller of property that the meeting to close the sale could take place as scheduled. While the associate was discussing one of the bank's comments on the drafts with the bank executive's assistant, the assistant mentioned that unanticipated problems had arisen in one of the property transactions. The associate believed that the problems the assistant had described would cause that property transaction to fall through, or at least not close as scheduled in that meeting.

The associate, running short on time remaining before the banker's departure for the meeting — and otherwise feeling hopelessly pressured by competing deadlines — decided not to revise and complete those documents relating to the problem transaction, but sent a folder containing the documents on the other transactions to the bank executive by courier. The executive placed the folder in his briefcase without looking through it and caught the plane to the site of the meeting with the purchaser and the purchaser's representatives. The following day, the supervising attorney received an angry call from the bank executive. The executive believed that the purchaser would have executed *all* of the documents during the negotiations, including the documents on the problematic property — if they had been ready.

What went wrong?

Of course, the associate's decision not to include the documents on the problem property — based on the assumption that the client did not need them — was not the associate's decision to make. The associate should have followed up on the conversation with the assistant and contacted the bank executive to seek direction or clarification. If unable to reach the executive, the associate should have proceeded to complete all the documents and request assistance within the firm as needed to meet the deadline.

APPLYING THIS EXPECTATION TO YOUR RESPONSIBILITIES

Respond promptly.

Inform promptly of anticipated delay.

Ascertain your follow-up responsibilities.

---

§ 3.05 EXPECTATION NO. 10: ASK FOR FEEDBACK

Increasingly, firms conduct periodic client evaluation or review processes with selected clients after their matters are completed. They ask, "What are we doing well; where do we need to improve?" Asking clients and customers for their reactions to the service they have received is a common practice in many industries. Applied to law firms, it has several benefits: it shows the client that the lawyers want to deliver good responsive service, and it provides the lead attorney or liaison attorney with an opportunity to identify and correct problems and to deal with unforeseen contingencies.

A client's reaction to plans in a case can also be sought as part of the regular process of communicating team efforts and progress. It reinforces the client's sense of participation in resolving problems. In fact, many clients increasingly expect the lead counsel to consult them in the process of formulating strategy. They also expect the lawyer to follow instructions they give, unless discussed and modified. The lead attorney or liaison attorney should also probe for any client dissatisfaction that could be avoided with timely discussion and clarification or adjustment. Unless asked, a client may not mention an area in which service is, or is perceived as, poor.

Asking for feedback serves a marketing, as well as a maintenance or retention function and may prompt referrals to other departments of the firm. Frequently, a client is unaware of the firm's range of services and the lead attorney is unaware of the client's additional needs to which others in the firm can respond. Often clients ask for a recommendation of another lawyer or firm to take care of a different type of matter. When the supervising attorney informs the client that the firm regularly handles those matters, the client looks surprised and says, "I didn't know your firm does that." Some clients may have had no contact with lawyers outside of the single practice area or department consulted, and have never been taken on an office tour or told what the rest of the firm does.

Examine the form in Appendix C, Client Service Audit: Corporate Counsel's Evaluation. This interview sheet is designed to elicit the client's evaluation and comments on the team's service on its matter and specifically identifies what the client liked, did not like, and wants to see improved. You can use this checklist as you work on a matter to monitor the client's likely assessment of your performance in those areas relating to your project.

CONSIDER:

By referral from an outside advisor, an attorney receives an estate planning assignment for a doctor. While developing the estate plan, the attorney and client talk about a buy-sell arrangement with the doctor's partners. At the end of the estate planning process, the lawyer asks the client's reaction to the manner in which the service was provided. The lawyer discovers that the doctor would like to move the partnership's medical clinic closer to the main hospital used by the partners. The doctor had never mentioned this desire before because it did not occur to him that it would be of interest to an estate planning attorney. The lawyer explains that the firm has handled the purchase and construction of buildings for other clients and that perhaps the doctor and partners should consider building on raw land that is for sale near the hospital. The lawyer summarizes the process. A few days later, the doctor invites the lawyer to confer with the partners.

What went right?

Initiating discussion about the doctor's satisfaction with the estate planning service resulted in additional financial benefit to the medical group and to the law firm. The medical group decided to build. Using the expertise of several firm lawyers throughout the process, the lawyer coordinated the project from zoning to tenant leases.

APPLYING THIS EXPECTATION TO YOUR RESPONSIBILITIES

How would the client respond if evaluating your performance?

Where are you doing well?

How can you improve?

Read one or more client survey checklists.

---

§ 3.06 EXPECTATION NO. 11: USE THE CLIENT'S LANGUAGE

Attorneys must be constantly aware that they are delivering a service — information in useful form, judgment, and recommendations — to clients who have specific objectives and distinctive operating styles, language, and jargon. Thus, for regular communication to be meaningful to the client, lawyers must 1) communicate what they are doing in language that the clients will understand, and 2) explain the benefits or effect of a development in terms of its impact on the ultimate objective. For example, because correspondence with another lawyer may be unintelligible to a nonlawyer, consider whether to attach an explanatory cover letter or note to the client's copy.

When in conference with a client through its corporate counsel and the company's business people, it is important to relate effectively to the business people as well as to the lawyers. The business people have been included in the meeting at someone's invitation for a reason. They expect and deserve your attention, too. Find out their respective involvement and roles in the matter so that you can appropriately interact with them. *See* § 6.07 [Part II, Expectation No. 8: "Develop Meeting and Telephone Skills"]. Also keep in mind that corporate counsel frequently ask their business people to evaluate the service performed by outside lawyers. Their opinions are important to corporate counsel; *they* are corporate counsel's clients.

If your work product is intended for the client, structure it so that the client can readily understand the significance of your answers and can use the information to take action, assess business risks, or make a decision. Spell out the options before relating the analysis of how each was developed. Put yourself in the client's place as you write and make presentations: think of the benefits before describing the features. Clients — as distinguished from your supervising attorneys — are generally uninterested in the process you follow in conducting an analysis. Instead, clients focus on how your recommendations or efforts move them toward their goals. *See* § 6.06 [Part II, Expectation No. 7: "Make Your Work Product Useful"].

APPLYING THIS EXPECTATION TO YOUR RESPONSIBILITIES

Place yourself in the client's position:

When communicating with a client, explain what you are doing in language the client understands.

Relate your advice or response to the client's goal.

Communicate options before the analysis.

Describe benefits as well as features.

---

§ 3.07 EXPECTATION NO. 12: COORDINATE SERVICE

Concern over coordination of services is typified by one client's comment, "I'm tired of paying for the same letter twice." Although they are aware and appreciative that the "best and the brightest" in a firm are working on their cases, clients often experience frustration and are confused and doubtful about the management of the "legal team" doing the work. A client's comment that "there are too many hands on the file" often stems from poor internal management and coordination of work, and duplicative assignments or responsibilities. A client expects the firm to manage and coordinate its legal services on each matter, and assumes that the firm has an effective internal system to do so. The client expects the lead attorney to be ultimately responsible for managing the firm's efforts and communicating with the client. The client wishes neither to manage the division of responsibilities within a firm nor to worry about accruing costs of duplicative legal services.

To efficiently handle the project and report progress to the client in a timely fashion, team members must communicate effectively among themselves. Client confidence in the firm's "legal team" builds as its work reflects consistent understanding and sensitivity to the client's ultimate objective and concerns. Conversely, client dissatisfaction with service looms if the client contacts an attorney to find out the status of a matter only to discover that the attorney is unable to respond because the project is being handled by another attorney unknown to the client. When more than one attorney — or an attorney and a legal assistant — are working on a matter, the team must be clear about the division of work. For example, junior attorneys should clarify whether they have signature authority for correspondence they prepare or whether it should go out over a senior associate's or partner's signature. Clients can become confused and irritated if they receive correspondence from unfamiliar names. Clients who are corporate counsel increasingly require outside counsel to obtain advance approval of each individual who will work on a matter. Corporate counsel often require an explanation of the expertise and roles of each attorney involved, billing rates, and expected time necessary to handle the matter. These specifics must be discussed among members of the legal team, and carried out consistently throughout the team's work on each matter.

Things to think about

- What are some features of your firm's, department's, or working group's system to manage work on a matter?
- What is the best way for team members to communicate with each other on complex matters? Periodic meetings? *Ad hoc* discussions as problems arise? Electronic mail?
- How often have you researched or prepared a document only to discover that the assignment had been completed by someone else hours or days earlier or was no longer needed?
- How often has your secretary or a legal assistant come to you having completed an assignment you took care of on the phone the day before?

Periodic meetings among members of the team assigned to a complex matter can be beneficial. If such sessions are scheduled in advance, with an agenda distributed before the meeting (*see* Appendix H, "Worksheet for Meeting Preparation"), members are more likely to prepare, present problems and developments, and ask for information they require in order of importance. A "case flow" or "case status" sheet helps direct and maintain the focus of these discussions. This sheet can illustrate the status of each team member's work on the case and planned actions — "To Do's" and timetables — from the last meeting. This allows the lead or supervising attorney to effectively guide discussion of the matter, to request each person to present a summary of his or her activities since the last meeting, and to propose future courses of action. The lead attorney can then provide new information and direction, and make suggestions.

If the lead attorney's secretary or legal assistant attends the meetings and then drafts minutes of the items discussed, each team member will have a working status report of all actions on the matter. Moreover, that secretary or legal assistant can serve as the point person for disseminating information about material changes in a matter if each team member communicates updates on status for distribution to the point person.

Close coordination is especially necessary when an attorney interviews for and brings in outside assistance on a project. The attorney must then integrate the outsider's efforts and communicate them to the client. For example, a client who is a defendant in an action requests the attorney to inquire whether an accounting firm would be interested in providing financial consulting and litigation support services on the case. The attorney helps the client establish selection criteria, reviews the responses of the various firms contacted, and advises the client on the selection. After the client makes its selection, the attorney coordinates the accounting firm's work regarding pretrial preparation.

If a client's advisor is involved — for example, the client's CPA — the supervising attorney or another attorney assigned to the matter should clarify appropriate coordination procedures with the client. If the client instructs the lawyer to work directly with its advisor, the lawyer ought to confirm the instruction in a letter to that advisor and copy the client. Sometimes legal work on an aspect of a matter affects work performed by the client's other nonlegal advisors. The client may seek the nonlegal advisor's opinion of the attorney's recommendation. Or, it may become prudent for the lawyer to seek the client's agreement to discuss the proposal with the nonlegal advisor.

CONSIDER:

The client's chief financial officer [CFO] and vice president for human resources are discussing with the lawyers various kinds of incentive compensation plans, including cash awards, stock grants, and stock options. The lawyers are recommending adoption of a stock grant plan they have structured. The CFO mentions that he wants to discuss the accounting impact of the ideas with the company's outside accounting firm.

Should the lawyers offer to call the accountants directly to discuss the recommendation? Have the lawyers worked with the accountants before? What is the CFO's predisposition and reaction to the idea? Do the lawyers believe that the CFO will deliver their recommendation and reasoning accurately?

Comments:

If the lawyers are concerned that the accountants may second-guess the recommendation, they may want to tactfully arrange to talk with the accountants so any objections or concerns they have regarding the recommendation can be addressed. Or, through a discussion of the company's other business plans, the lawyers may position themselves to discuss and develop modifications to the plan.

When interacting with members of the client's staff, treat them with respect and be sensitive to their positions. They are resources, not subordinates. Suppose, for example, an insurance company adjuster's assignment was to take statements of the witnesses before suit was filed and you, as trial counsel, became involved. You review the file and determine that the adjuster should have interviewed and taken a statement of a certain witness.

Would you call the adjuster's supervisor or a staff attorney for the insurance company? It may be more appropriate to telephone the adjuster and ask that the witness be interviewed, instead of calling the in-house lawyer or firing off a letter saying that there is no statement from Mr. White in the file and that his statement needs to be taken. The adjuster reports to a superior and will be concerned about a letter reflecting poorly on his or her preparation. You or your firm will probably work with that adjuster again. Strive to build a good working relationship with each of the persons with whom you work. That adjuster may move around but his moves will probably be within the industry. He could become an important source of new business. Similarly, peers in other organizations may become decision makers there or elsewhere in a few years.

CONSIDER:

While preparing for a real estate closing, a lawyer spots a problem with the mortgage balance listed by the seller's mortgage company. The lawyer discusses the error with a vice president of the mortgage company with whom she has been dealing and, together with the client's mortgage company, resolves it. The vice president will not attend the closing but assures the attorney that he will relay the resolution to the mortgage officer handling the closing details. Would you take any additional steps?

This attorney also called the mortgage officer to confirm the instructions and to ensure the appropriate adjustments were being made to the draft document. The closing proceeded smoothly.

APPLYING THIS EXPECTATION TO YOUR RESPONSIBILITIES

Know:

Each team member's section of the work.

With whom you are expected to coordinate your work.

How frequently you are expected to coordinate your work.

The agenda for case review or case flow meetings.

4

In the Real World: Translating Legal Work into Client Service

§ 4.01 EXPECTATIONS THIRTEEN THROUGH TWENTY

Clients expect their lawyers to:

No. 13 Understand the client's business.

No. 14 Consider the practical aspects.

No. 15 Spot related problems.

No. 16 Design responsive solutions.

No. 17 Use economic sense.

No. 18 Serve as a resource.

No. 19 Update the client on new legal developments and techniques.

No. 20 Understand the expectations of a corporate law department.

§ 4.02 EXPECTATION NO. 13: UNDERSTAND THE CLIENT'S BUSINESS

A client's goals and expectations do not exist in a vacuum. Client expectations arise from real business objectives, opportunities, operations, problems, company idiosyncrasies, and psychological needs. Just as the practice of law involves terms of art and familiarity with a particular court's perspective, other businesses have their own specialized customs, terms, and acronyms. Lawyers who desire to translate their legal skills into excellent client service must become appropriately familiar with the client, and the client's company and industry. This familiarity serves three purposes: (1) conversance with the client's language, perspective, and strategies; (2) recognition and analysis of problems peculiar to that business; and (3) anticipation and understanding of the context and trends shaping the client's goals, priorities, and frame of reference. The degree of familiarity needed varies for regular or full service and for transactional legal service.

CONSIDER:

A client manufacturing company pays royalties to the licensor under a contract that the lawyer drafted two years ago. In the contract, the royalty percentages are lower for goods which are sold at a discount, up to a certain volume of sales. The volume of discount sales that qualifies for the lower rate was close to the company's actual volume of discount sales at the time the contract became effective.

The company's vice president of finance has just conducted an analysis of profit margins for each of the company's lines. Recent competitiveness in the industry has forced more design risks than ever before and, therefore, many of the goods will be sold at a discount. The company wants to continue doing business with the licensor but wants its relationship to reflect these changes in the industry. The contract is about to expire and the president sends it to the lawyer, requesting that he "update the contract."

Actual result

The attorney revised only the expiration terms in the contract and sent it over to the company for the president's signature. The president gave it to the vice president of finance to review.

What went wrong?

The lawyer failed to consider information and perspectives he had gained from other projects regarding the impact of increased competition upon the company. He also failed to consider adjustments he knew thc company was making to maintain its market strength. The attorney should have conferred with the client to determine its current goals relative to this contract and to develop a creative contractual solution to increase either the volume or categories of discount sales that would qualify for the lower royalty rate in exchange for a concession in another area.

How can you develop your practical knowledge about a client's business and industry? If the client is a publicly held company, read over its annual report, financial statements, proxy disclosures, and so forth. For example, you can learn about the background of each member of the board of directors from information contained in proxy disclosure material. To gain knowledge of an industry's chief executive officers [CEOs], practices, problems, and trends, and to amass information about your firm's clients and their competitors, peruse local business magazines and newspapers, national business magazines, industry trade journals, the *Wall Street Journal,* the business section of the *New York Times,* and similar publications. Becoming familiar with an industry will also help you to recognize marketing opportunities later as you undertake business development responsibilities.

A third year associate in a firm that represents a number of hospitals and physicians developed a personal program to gain more practical knowledge about the health care industry; it may provide some ideas. Over a three month period, the associate planned to: (1) list friends and acquaintances who are employed in or who service this industry, such as those holding positions in hospitals, pharmaceutical companies, health maintenance organizations [HMOs], public relations people, brokers, and bankers; (2) contact these people and learn their opinions about the industry's technological developments, current practices, concerns, and trends; (3) learn industry jargon; (4) discover which industry associations are composed of upper and middle management people — those who are decision-makers and influencers in purchasing legal services; (5) attend an industrial association meeting with an acquaintance who belongs to that association; and (6) subscribe to a leading trade newsletter or journal.

Modest though these steps may appear, they enabled this associate to develop information and a network of resources within the health care profession. When meeting with a client, this associate can now comfortably discuss various developments and concerns affecting the client, the community, and the industry. The associate can also demonstrate familiarity with the way the client conducts business, to reinforce the client's confidence in the firm team. These efforts will serve as the foundation for recognizing opportunities for marketing the firm's services in the industry when developing an individual marketing action plan [MAP^{SM}].

Occasionally it is desirable to visit the client's offices to gain an appreciation of its business cycle, working environment, and operational structure. Many senior executives and entrepreneurs are delighted when outside advisors see "their team" in action. A vice president of finance for a manufacturing company put it this way: "I want lawyers and accountants to come to our plant and see what kind of a monster I'm driving!" Given the positive reception and results of such trips, many executives are expecting — if not demanding — such attention. Therefore, if you have been working directly with your counterparts in a client organization, consider the appropriateness of arranging an on-site meeting or visit.

Sometimes, of course, a trip to an adversary's plant is a crucial part of preparation. In one situation, a lawyer defending a contract claim concerning component parts the client supplied to the plaintiff visited the plaintiff's manufacturing plant. As a result of this trip, the lawyer found some holes in the plaintiff's case and developed a creative trial strategy that resulted in a substantial reduction of that plaintiff's recovery.

APPLYING THIS EXPECTATION TO YOUR RESPONSIBILITIES

Acquire practical knowledge about key client businesses and industries, including:

Industry trends affecting client objectives.

Problems particular to that industry.

Business and financial jargon.

Products, services, market shares, industry leaders.

Gather insight and information from peers in the industry.

Become familiar with industry associations and trade journals.

---

§ 4.03 EXPECTATION NO. 14: CONSIDER THE PRACTICAL ASPECTS

Inexperienced attorneys often overlook a central client expectation: that the attorney will view the client's objective or problem from several angles, grasp the essence of the matter, and develop workable options to achieve the result desired. Workable options are grounded on practical, as well as legal, considerations. ABA Model Rule 2.1 recognizes this: "In rendering advice, a lawyer may refer not only to law but to other considerations such as moral, economic, social and political factors, that may be relevant to the client's situation."

An ability to cut through tangential issues quickly and incisively is particularly crucial where the matter requires prompt attention and managing momentum is paramount. Thoughtful inquiries and sensitivity to the practical ramifications of legal advice foster a useful work product for both the supervising attorney and the client. Too often new attorneys, unskilled at viewing an objective from the client's perspective, launch into a detailed analysis of legal issues but fail to focus on the client's goal or problem. This tendency has been described by the well-worn phrase, "These are the subtleties in which only lawyers get lost."

CONSIDER:

A client who represents various auto parts manufacturers asks his attorney to analyze a proposed arrangement between a group of wholesale "jobbers" and himself. The client wants to set up contracts with the jobbers for purchasing parts from his various manufacturers. The proposed "full service purchase contracts" would allow the jobbers to purchase the parts at a special discount so long as they use only the manufacturers connected with the client.

The attorney advises the client against undertaking this business arrangement with the jobbers because the contracts would likely be construed as tying arrangements in violation of antitrust laws. The client's unspoken and unhappy reaction is: "My attorney does not understand that this is a valuable business opportunity. Surely there is a way to do it." To do what?

What went wrong?

Because the attorney viewed the problem as an isolated legal question, he was oblivious to the value the client placed on having a relationship with these jobbers. The attorney's "advice" made legal sense, but business nonsense.

What alternatives to a binding contract would accomplish the client's goal of encouraging the jobbers to do most of their business with him? The attorney could have asked the client what types of incentives would attract the jobbers. After discussing how the client might provide value to the jobbers, the attorney might have suggested and then structured an incentive arrangement to accomplish the client's purpose without running the risk of violating antitrust laws.

Comment:

Suppose, for liability reasons, a client prefers a limited partnership to run a family real estate operation. During the discussions, the client mentions that the family members are very close and confer about most business and investment options before making any decisions. The lawyer should ask whether the family members who would be limited partners would be content to leave the day-to-day affairs of the business to the full partners to manage.

In these situations, you must pay attention to both the practical and the legal considerations. Note also that the lead counsel will frequently recommend to the client that they consult another professional advisor for an assessment of factors related to that professional's area of expertise. Examples of consultants that may be needed include: an accountant to help determine the costs of a undertaking a project and/or the costs of delays in its completion, an appraiser to help in evaluating a purchase price, and a construction expert or an engineer to help determine the feasibility of a scheduled completion date for a project.

APPLYING THIS EXPECTATION TO YOUR RESPONSIBILITIES

Anticipate and consider the practical ramifications of each alternative strategy and of your recommendations. Check to ensure they are consistent with:

Client's business objective.

Client's evaluation of what is at stake.

---

§ 4.04 EXPECTATION NO. 15: SPOT RELATED PROBLEMS

Lawyers must continually evaluate whether and how legal issues outside of their "practice areas" affect a transaction. For example, a bankruptcy lawyer's role in corporate policies and strategy may extend to tax, real estate, labor relations, and transactional work such as acquisitions and mergers. New lawyers often must train themselves to become sensitive to this expectation because law school courses generally do not train students to spot problems outside of the subject matter of a course. Indeed, law students studiously ignore substantive or procedural issues beyond the purview of the course: professors do not give points for discussing tort issues in a contracts final exam. Conversely, an attorney must focus both narrowly and broadly on the client's objectives to recognize related problems. The ability to recognize companion or tangential problems is as often dependent upon understanding the context of a client's concern or question as it is a function of paying attention to the details of a transaction.

Periodic in-house continuing legal education sessions held by firm members from other practice areas help attune inexperienced lawyers to recurring interrelationships among practice areas and to formation of new informal working or practice groups that specialize in specific client needs or transactions. For example, servicing entrepreneurial high technology businesses and businesses engaging in international trade requires a team that cuts across traditional departmental boundaries.

APPLYING THIS EXPECTATION TO YOUR RESPONSIBILITIES

Become familiar with interrelationships among practice areas on key types of client matters.

List recurring client objectives, problems, and issues which cut across those areas of legal expertise.

What are effective methods of coordinating team work among practice areas?

---

§ 4.05 EXPECTATION NO. 16: DESIGN RESPONSIVE SOLUTIONS

Clients expect their attorneys to find ways to achieve their goals or solve their problems. When a client asks if something can be done and the lawyer determines that it cannot, the next question – whether or not articulated – usually is, "Then, how can I do it?" A client's objectives or problems seldom are tidily packaged; instead, client priorities, preferences, and factual circumstances demand creative thought throughout the process to determine workable options and to reach the best solution.

Creative problem solving is not synonymous with taking shortcuts in legal research and analysis. The creative lawyer is just as thorough and as meticulous as his or her colleagues. The creative lawyer, however, listens to the client carefully during the engagement process to understand what the client wants to do, maintains a consistent focus on the client's overall objective and priorities, communicates with the client, and then designs a responsive, workable solution.

CONSIDER:

A lawyer represents a client who is forming a corporation in which she owns 60 percent of the stock. The client wants to control the day-to-day operations but she also wants to motivate the minority shareholders to take an interest in planning major corporate policies, such as new markets and growth issues. The client asks the lawyer to design a mechanism to help accomplish both of these objectives. How would you draft the majority and minority voting rights to achieve this result?

A Solution:

The lawyer drafts a provision that requires only a simple majority of stock ownership for a vote to set the number of directors and to elect them. A 75 percent vote is required on certain other significant issues. The lawyer confers with the client to develop a list of these significant issues and then attends the meeting in which the client and minority shareholders agree on the issues. This solution enables the client to run the day-to-day operations; the voting rights design ensures that the client can continue business operations even if there is a disagreement among shareholders. The design also encourages the minority shareholders to maintain their interest in addressing the policy-making and strategic planning aspects of the business because their votes are required to change or implement certain policies.

APPLYING THIS EXPECTATION TO YOUR RESPONSIBILITIES

Adopt a can-do attitude.

You can more effectively develop responsive, workable solutions if you:

Step back periodically. Ask yourself why you are doing what you are doing.

Question your assumptions.

Devise and assess alternative means to reach the client's goal.

Consider cost-effectiveness as well as risks of each alternative.

---

§ 4.06 EXPECTATION NO. 17: USE ECONOMIC SENSE

Clients expect that their legal matters will be handled efficiently as well as effectively and that their lawyers will think in terms of what makes sense economically – that is, "How long will it take? How much will it cost?" No longer satisfactory, with limited exceptions, is the attitude "do the job well regardless of cost." Many clients may be unfamiliar with technical legal nuances, but they do know when the numbers work and when they do not make sense. Usually a client is not interested in attaining an "optimal result at all cost." If the client refuses to pay or the responsible attorney cuts inappropriately spent time, the firm will pay for that written-down time.

As discussed earlier (§§ 2.05-2.07 [Part I, Expectations Nos. 4-6]), establishing the ground rules for an engagement during the engagement process goes a long way toward preventing unpleasant surprises later because of assumptions the client has made about "how long it will take" and "how much it will cost." Adhering to the terms in the engagement letter and contacting the client when departures from prior estimates are needed is one way lawyers demonstrate to a client their economic sense in concert with professional judgment in day-to-day work. This must be coupled with sensitivity to the client's need to control fees and costs. If a fee or engagement letter is available, its terms may cover several areas that provide the context for the new lawyer's assignment. These areas may include:

- Objective
- Scope (and limits) of service
- What is expected of the client
- Particulars of the fee arrangement
- Staffing requirements, qualifications, and billing rate(s)
- Arrangements for billing expenses — retainer; third party to bill client directly; include in regular bill or bill separately from fees
- Payment terms — billing interval; service charge

Lawyers are expected to watch and monitor the cumulative cost-effectiveness of time spent and expenses in light of estimates of the probable amount of recovery, the amount in controversy, the budget allocated to the matter, or the value to the client of reaching the objective according to an appropriate measure — cash? Present value? This does not mean to apply a cut and dried formula, but rather to consider the problem from the client's perspective while assessing what actions and strategy are most cost-effective.

If the associate's path to the desired objective or result becomes less cost-effective than was earlier discussed, it is up to him or her to inform the supervising attorney. *See* § 6.05 [Part II, Expectation No. 6: "Communicate Progress and Status"]. Then the supervising attorney, together with the client, can timely reassess the value of the goal, and consider alternative means of reaching it. They can also discuss the appropriateness of modifying the goal.

CONSIDER:

A law firm's assignment is to evict several delinquent commercial tenants and to pursue collection of rents. The assigned lawyer discovers that the efforts against one of the tenants have become more costly than projected and alerts the supervising attorney, who in turn alerts the client. The client and supervising attorney review the status of each of the cases and the overall budget, and evaluate whether to continue recovery efforts against that tenant.

Here, the client appreciated the lawyer calling the issue of cost to his attention; had the client discovered the problem on the statement of fees when the costs were out of balance with the projected amount of recovery, the client could have concluded that the supervising lawyer had little financial sense, did not manage the cases, or was interested in only one thing: billing time – fees – regardless of whether continued work made sense to the client.

Clients expect their bills to reflect the value of the lawyer's efforts. Good clients object to and resent fees for which there is little demonstrated increase in value. Without some explanation by the lawyer, the client who is uninvolved in the day-to-day activity may not recognize the significance of each activity — meetings, memoranda, telephone calls — and how they collectively contribute to reaching the objective or solving the problem. Consistent communication of effort and progress made should eliminate surprise when the client reviews the statement for professional services.

When describing your time, put yourself in the client's place. If you were paying for your services, how would you best describe them? Clients want to see descriptions of items that they, as businessmen, understand. Also consider the billing attorney: he or she needs to understand what work you have done to determine how to bill it. A concise description that requires little rewording will be appreciated, if not expected.

The lawyer can also provide guidance by making periodic telephone calls, by writing notes on copies of correspondence sent to the client, and by sending and discussing status reports shortly before the client receives a bill. A lawyer has an obligation to evaluate the relative cost-effectiveness of allocating firm resources and outside resources in a matter. Examples include comparing the costs and relative value of available experts, carefully assessing whether more than one lawyer is needed at a meeting, hearing, or deposition, and cost-effective use of legal assistants, computerized research, automated litigation support, and so forth.

CONSIDER:

You are assigned work for both a corporation and, personally, for its chief executive officer, the majority shareholder. You are aware that minority shareholders in this closely-held corporation have fought with the managing majority shareholder during the last two years over a variety of issues, including the reasonableness of certain major expenditures.

How would you describe your time for the services performed for the corporation and the services performed for the CEO?

In this case, the associate clearly delineated time spent on corporation business and time spent on the CEO's personal matters. This enabled the billing attorney to easily prepare a separate bill for the personal work to discourage any suggestion by a disgruntled shareholder or the IRS that the CEO did not distinguish personal legal work from corporate legal work. The separate bill was used by the bookkeeping department to calculate additional W-2 income for the CEO. The billing attorney also wrote a cover letter transmitting the bill, which explained why separate bills were prepared.

The advice an attorney gives to a client must make financial sense to the client in the context of that client's business or personal affairs. If the client expects little available cash for the remainder of the year because of expansion plans, then structuring a real estate acquisition that contemplates cash to finance a large portion of the price would be incompatible with the realities of the client's financial situation and other plans. If the lawyer asks questions and focuses on the financial picture, other means of acquisition can be explored, such as an exchange of properties.

CONSIDER:

A manufacturer needs to purchase raw material requirements on credit for the next six months. You are involved in structuring the credit arrangements with a group of banks.

What would you ask about the industry practice, the company's past and existing arrangements, and the banks' position on payment for raw materials?

Comment:

In this case, payment was required to ship each order. A postponed shipment because of delay in payment would have disrupted manufacture of samples for the largest seasonal trade show. The lawyer who handled this transaction obtained this information along with the requirements for cumulative credit for the next six months. The lawyer recognized that the negotiations had to be completed before the first scheduled shipping date of the raw materials. This lawyer demonstrated practical financial sensitivity to the imperative of shipping on time to avoid jeopardizing the marketing of the seasonal product.

APPLYING THIS EXPECTATION TO YOUR RESPONSIBILITIES

Comply with terms of the engagement/fee letter.

Monitor cumulative cost-effectiveness of your efforts and expenses in reaching the objective.

Notify the supervising attorney if you find your course of action will exceed estimates or is becoming less cost-effective than was discussed. Be prepared to propose alternatives, as appropriate.

Prepare billing descriptions that make sense to the supervising attorney and client.

---

§ 4.07 EXPECTATION NO. 18: SERVE AS A RESOURCE

In the typical attorney-client relationship, the attorney is called upon to service clients on an *ad hoc* or transactional basis. There are times, however, when a client wants the lawyer's expertise as a resource or sounding board for preliminary ideas or strategy. For example, an entrepreneur offers financial services to clients. He does not want to internally staff certain professional positions because their advice is not required daily. Outside advisors, including attorneys, are well suited to serve as resources, however, because of their independence and exposure to creative planning opportunities. So the company retains a team of experts representing various professions to ensure that its clients receive the best thinking on all aspects of a proposed financial design. The team consists of an attorney, a CPA, an actuary, a financial analyst, and a management consultant. As a primary resource, the attorney's value and role is to evaluate ideas and to brainstorm preliminary design ideas from a practical as well as a legal perspective. This allows the company's management group to think through ideas early on, eliminate unworkable approaches, and to focus on those with merit. Later, in the process of refining a proposed plan, the attorney is again called upon to analyze specific elements and to prepare the documents.

CONSIDER:

A financial corporation decides to establish a program to help its employees prepare for retirement. The employee relations department designs a two-day seminar to cover various retirement planning areas, and puts together a panel of speakers to address each area. The speakers include a representative from the Social Security Administration, a physician, an in-house employee benefits analyst, an insurance representative, a financial manager, a retired employee, and an estate planning attorney.

Comment:

The estate planner should contact the in-house employee benefits analyst to become familiar with the company's retirement plan and any other relevant benefits so that the presentation can be tailored to address the practical questions and concerns of that group. This project serves as a marketing tool because some employees may need specialized advice, wills, or trusts. (The attorney may speak for a fee or may intend it solely as a promotional opportunity.)

APPLYING THIS EXPECTATION TO YOUR RESPONSIBILITIES

Observe how the supervising attorney serves the client as a

Resource.

Sounding board for new ideas.

How does the supervising attorney "add value" to the relationship by serving in this role?

---

§ 4.08 EXPECTATION NO. 19: UPDATE CLIENTS ON NEW LEGAL DEVELOPMENTS AND TECHNIQUES

Successful clients strive to remain on the competitive edge of legal developments and techniques affecting their businesses. Thus, every attorney has a direct interest in informing his or her clients about new developments and techniques. Through such efforts the attorney can effectively build and maintain client confidence. Regularly updating clients reduces the possibility that information is miscommunicated by a colleague on the golf course or, worse, that the client learns of important information first through a loss to a competing company.

Learn to be sensitive to even the most casual inquiries by clients about legal developments, new legislation, or new techniques affecting their businesses. When a client expresses curiosity about or interest in pending legislation, use your own follow-up system to keep the client informed by telephone, personal correspondence, firm newsletter, or firm seminar. Similarly, a supervising attorney may assign legislative tracking or follow-up to you.

Communicate information in terms of opportunities or solutions to problems. You may have written an internal memorandum about new legislation, a new case, or a planning opportunity, or recently briefed an issue of general interest to a client. Consider whether circulating this information to clients would be appropriate (after deleting any confidential references). This technique serves a marketing function as well. The information you circulate may be useful to lawyers in a client's law department and will keep your firm's presence in mind. Your firm newsletter is useful to a client if it gives practical information about new laws or recent decisions affecting the client's industry.

APPLYING THIS EXPECTATION TO YOUR RESPONSIBILITIES

Flag information to update clients on significant:

Pending legislation.

New case law.

Planning opportunities.

Communicate in terms that are meaningful to the client.

Contribute developments of interest to a group of clients to your firm's client newsletter.

---

§ 4.09 EXPECTATION NO. 20: UNDERSTAND THE EXPECTATIONS OF A CORPORATE LAW DEPARTMENT

How do the client expectations discussed in Part I apply when the client is the general counsel of a corporation or another attorney in its law department? Although you will find that in-house counsel generally share the expectations held by other clients, some differences exist because they hire outside lawyers to assist them in serving their client — the entire company and its various divisions. You will be able to better anticipate and respond to house counsels' expectations by understanding (1) their role and responsibilities in serving their client, and (2) some common purposes for which they seek outside assistance.

§ 4.09(a) Law Department's Role

The law department is responsible for handling the company's legal affairs. Its lawyers provide legal advice and assistance to the company to reach its business objectives and to make a reasonable profit for the shareholders. Senior management expects its lawyers to anticipate problems and develop preventive measures, and to solve existing problems. Their advice must reflect an understanding of the business objectives, philosophy, procedures, personnel, and economic problems and opportunities the business and industry face. House counsel are also expected to maximize cost saving techniques.

§ 4.09(b) Use of Outside Lawyers

House counsels' use of outside attorneys varies tremendously from company to company and from matter to matter. A firm may be retained, for example, to handle complex litigation requiring multidiscipline expertise or litigation that arises in a foreign jurisdiction.

CONSIDER:

The corporation was sued in a rural county court of a distant state for many millions of dollars. Its law department handles the company's regulatory work and local litigation. Due to staffing constraints and lack of familiarity with that state's laws and rules of procedural practice, the law department sought outside counsel to handle the day-to-day strategy and preparation of this case.

The law department attorney assigned to the case engaged as lead counsel a lawyer in that state who had handled a previous matter well for the company and whose law firm possessed appropriate substantive expertise and depth. The inside lawyer asked for references to guide the selection of local counsel in that county. Lead outside counsel recommended a firm of three lawyers with whom he had worked. Local counsel was expected to keep the law department and lead outside counsel abreast of local rules and unwritten practices in the county.

A firm will likely be called upon to assist in high profile matters in which the company faces a substantial risk of adverse publicity. When an issue arises on which the company has substantial financial exposure, senior management, the board of directors, and the shareholders are concerned. The general counsel may engage an outside firm to provide a second opinion for protective purposes. A law department attorney, although possessing the necessary technical expertise or theoretical knowledge, may call upon an outside lawyer to structure a transaction if the department lacks the outside lawyer's practical familiarity with industry-wide or foreign business practices involved in similar transactions. Or, when faced with an unanticipated volume of cases, inside counsel may seek assistance periodically to ease workload constraints. Increases in workload may also prompt house counsel to enlarge the scope of an assignment delegated to outside lawyers. For example, a firm has been engaged to provide technical assistance in a transaction. Shortly after making the assignment, the assistant general counsel who is in charge of that transaction found it essential to devote his attention to a difficult litigation matter. As a result, he requested the outside lawyer to undertake a larger role in the transaction.

In some situations, inside counsel desires *ad hoc* advice and will use outside lawyers as a sounding board and confidant. They want a devil's advocate who will probe into the basis for their reasoning. For example, during a rapid development of events, house counsel may seek assistance to assess risks, to answer senior management's questions — "What if we do this . . . what if we do that?" — and to formulate workable solutions to limit the company's exposure. Outside lawyers may be an invaluable sounding board because they possess broad-based familiarity with how an administrative agency or a foreign government is dealing with an issue generally throughout the industry. An inside counsel is less likely to know what new position a regulatory agency has begun asserting against its competitors which would also impact its own proposed plans.

§ 4.09(c) Selection of Outside Counsel

Often, outside lawyers are selected on the basis of a recommendation by an attorney in the law department who has used them or by a colleague in another company. Sometimes inside lawyers choose a lawyer who they have observed across the table negotiating on behalf of another party to a transaction or in the courtroom representing an adversary. Referrals are also often made by other law firms. The lead firm on a case may recommend a lawyer with another firm to act as local counsel or to handle a matter outside of its areas of expertise. The criteria that the law department uses to choose an outside lawyer may extend beyond that lawyer's expertise and personality. House counsel often inquire about the depth and qualifications of that lawyer's team members who will assist in the matter.

Note that more than one lawyer in a law department may be responsible for selection of outside counsel to assist in various types of matters. An assistant general counsel who directs regulatory compliance may seek a litigator's assistance; the attorney in charge of financing transactions may periodically retain a securities or tax lawyer. In another company the chief financial officer or treasurer may select an outside tax lawyer to handle a state tax controversy. Therefore, inquiry into the company's managerial structure and reporting channels may be required before a lawyer can successfully cross-sell a partner's services and facilitate appropriate introductions.

§ 4.09(d) Establishment of Engagement Ground Rules

House counsel usually have well defined expectations of outside counsel and of the ground rules that will govern the relationship. During the engagement process they discuss the goal and priorities, and ensure there is a common understanding of each issue. Together with the lead outside lawyer, they allocate responsibilities, develop a staffing plan to achieve optimal allocation of partner and associate roles, and set an initial timetable for major tasks. In most matters, inside counsel is very sensitive to controlling the costs estimated and incurred in reaching the desired result. House counsel often project fees and costs in creating a budget, and discuss billing procedures. Many companies track the billing history on ongoing matters, monitor cumulative costs against the budgeted amounts, and periodically re-evaluate the value of the matter, the exposure of the company, and the cost-effectiveness of outside legal services. Outside counsel who ignore cost projections and budgets will find the law department looking elsewhere for representation.

CONSIDER:

A law department attorney engaged a litigator to handle contractual litigation. Upon reviewing the files, the inside attorney realized that he and the litigator would have to meet with several managers based in the southeast and southwest regions. Because the company's busiest stretch in its business cycle would begin in two months, it would become increasingly difficult and expensive to bring these employees together. An opportunity arose for assembling the group at headquarters in three weeks. The inside lawyer contacted outside counsel and scheduled the meeting. At that meeting the litigation partner and an associate covered a few preliminary issues. Six weeks later the litigator requested that inside counsel schedule another meeting with these managers. Inside counsel believed that the information needed could have been obtained at the earlier meeting. He was displeased with the lawyer's apparent lack of sensitivity to costs and the managers' time. He unhappily anticipated the reaction that the operations department would have when reviewing the charge for the additional meeting against its budget: the vice president of operations may well perceive that the inside lawyer has been managing the case poorly.

What could the outside lawyer have done?

If the lawyer believed the first meeting was premature, he should have communicated his perception and reasoning to the inside counsel. Then, if the meeting was still held, the lawyer could have reiterated that they could work through some issues but that they would need to reconvene later depending on intervening developments.

§ 4.09(e) Teamwork

House counsel expect their staff attorneys and the outside lawyers to work as a team according to the roles and responsibilities agreed upon during the engagement process. Accessibility, regular communication, and coordination are key ingredients for effective team work.

Inside attorneys often need to get in touch with their counterparts quickly. They expect to work with lawyers who are accessible. Suppose, an inside attorney is directed to prepare and submit briefing papers for the company's board of directors by the end of the day. He calls the outside lawyer to find out the status of an analysis the firm lawyers are performing. Or the general counsel has called the partner to obtain an opinion on an aspect of a matter before meeting with the chief executive officer later that morning. If outside lawyers fail to return calls promptly in those situations, inside counsel will quickly become dissatisfied with their service. Some general counsels maintain a relationship with a liaison partner whom they expect to be accessible for periodic conferences on overall strategy and in emergencies, and to monitor the cost-effectiveness of the firm team's work. *See* § 2.04(h) [Part I, Expectation No. 3: "Determine the Role Each Lawyer Will Fill"] and Appendix C, Client Service Audit: Corporate Counsel's Evaluation.

Regular communication and coordination among the lawyers is necessary to carry out their respective responsibilities. For example, outside lawyers need assistance to obtain and assess information relating to the company's policies, procedures, personnel, and factual details. Suppose an associate is assigned to prepare a company employee for a deposition. By conferring with the in-house attorney first, the associate may be better able to anticipate potential trouble spots and to effectively prepare the witness.

To carry out their role of managing the outside legal work, corporate law department attorneys generally expect to be involved in assessing alternatives and creating solutions. In addition, they are familiar with their company's goals, business perspective, priorities, approach to weighing risks, and expectations. Communication is key in meeting inside counsel's expectations, in formulating a strategy and tactics that remain consistent with the company's related plans and activities, and in developing workable solutions. Suppose, for example, the corporation decides to improve the tone of its relationship with the adversary during the pendency of litigation due to a new business opportunity. The approach to the litigation will have to be adjusted accordingly.

You will probably experience early client contact with lawyers in the law department. As a member of the team, become attuned to the corporation's culture and operational style. Each corporate client is different and has distinct needs, goals, and management styles. Understand the inside lawyer's roles and responsibilities to the client and specific expectations held by the supervising attorney and client in this matter.

Your role and scope of work will vary with the type of matter and with the nature of the relationship between your firm and the company's general counsel — frequent service, a one-time assignment, or assistance in specialized matters. Whatever your specific role, generally your overall objective will be to assist those lawyers to manage and resolve the matter or legal problem. In carrying out your responsibilities, maintain a comfortable working relationship by adapting the expectations discussed in this Part I to the context of your teamwork with inside counsel.

APPLYING THIS EXPECTATION TO YOUR RESPONSIBILITIES

To apply Part I, Expectations of Clients in the context of an engagement by inside counsel, determine:

Supervising attorney's role.

Your role.

Role of your counterpart in the law department.

Ask Yourself: "Am I helping inside counsel manage and resolve this matter or legal problem?"

PART II

Expectations of Supervising Attorney

5

Balancing Professional and Business Responsibilities

§ 5.01 INTRODUCTION TO PART II, GENERALLY

The responsibility of new lawyers is to become able professionals. This requires the associate to learn about the firm's philosophy and policies and to demonstrate a "can-do," team-player attitude: in short, to assimilate oneself into the firm. It also requires the associate to develop the professional judgment that is essential to the delivery of excellent client service and legal research and analysis.

Partners' expectations of associate attorneys are influenced by clients' and the firm's expectations of partners. Supervising attorneys, the associate's immediate "clients," are accountable to firm clients for the delivery of excellent legal service. A supervising attorney, in turn, expects and requires the assigned associate attorney to demonstrate excellence in work product, service to client and community, and enjoyment of practice and relationships with colleagues.

The new associate expects to receive quality training from the firm. The associate, however, must take the initiative to discover what the firm, supervising attorneys, and their clients expect of each other; and then, to learn how to perform practical tasks that extend beyond an academic notion of "legal work" to encompass the operation of the practice both as a business and as a profession.

Part II is intended to provide the associate with some of the direction that is frequently missing or sporadically given in the associate's "rookie" year, to assist each in adopting an effective "workstyle": a style of practicing law that is imbued with goals, guidelines, routines, tools, and an understanding of the practice as a business.

APPLYING THIS EXPECTATION TO YOUR RESPONSIBILITIES

Supervising attorneys expect you to:

1. Attune yourself to the profession and to the business.
2. Understand and clarify assignments.
3. Manage your workload and time.

4. Manage your assignments.
5. Stay on track by thinking broadly and narrowly.
6. Communicate progress and status.
7. Produce a useful work product.
8. Develop meeting and telephone skills.
9. Plan your career.
10. Lay the foundation for business development.

---

§ 5.02 EXPECTATION NO. 1: ATTUNE YOURSELF TO THE PROFESSION AND TO THE BUSINESS

Whatever your practice, as a lawyer you do more than dispense a service that is predesigned or is measurable by concrete criteria. You cannot simply look up rules and plug in "what is right." Instead, you must use technical expertise and apply judgment to determine how to best achieve each client's goal. The process you follow in delivering legal service, and the result reached, will define the quality of your representation of the client, and your reputation in your firm and the profession.

Therefore, as new lawyers refine analytical skills and technical competence, they face these additional obligations: to set a course to build professional judgment — a unique and crucial resource to a client — and to become attuned to economic realities affecting their firms.

§ 5.02(a) Professionalism

That a lawyer possesses professional values is the expectation shared by the firm, the public, clients, and supervising attorneys — the foundation of the legal profession.

Key to developing professional judgment is adherence to principles of professional conduct. Professional conduct encompasses ethical responsibilities and legal etiquette. The self-discipline and dedication with which each lawyer adheres to the principles of professional conduct is also the touchstone of whether the profession will be accorded the privilege of remaining self-regulated.

Although most completed a course in legal ethics as law students, new associates will find it essential to review ethics principles regularly as they encounter and work through real problems. Ethical responsibilities that affect assignments from the inception of practice include: confidentiality, attorney-client privilege, identification of potential conflicts, supervision of nonlawyer assistants, advocacy principles, and trial conduct. For example, a common conflicts situation occurs if an employee of the firm's corporate client suddenly asks for advice in pursuing a course of action inconsistent with corporate interests and policies. Litigators must also review Fed. R. Civ. P. 11 (and any state version), and new opinions interpreting it, which requires any lawyer filing papers in federal court to make reasonable inquiry as to whether the papers are "well-grounded in fact," and are supported by existing law or by a "good faith" basis to justify credible argument to reverse or to modify existing law. Lawyers certify by their signatures that the paper is not filed to delay, harass, or increase the expense of the litigation.

Professionalism contemplates attention to "common sense" rules of etiquette and protocol. Frequently, discovery practices reveal a lawyer's flagrant breach of etiquette toward other lawyers, witnesses, or court reporters. For example, a medical doctor informed a state's grievance committee that the lawyer who took his deposition refused to address him as "Doctor!" Seemingly losing ground in today's world, yet an invaluable business commodity and ingredient of professional conduct, is being courteous. Examples of courtesies too often forgotten include:

- Courtesy to the clerk and other court personnel
- Courteous behavior to a client's employees
- Punctuality
- Holding nonemergency calls until the conclusion of a meeting
- Prompt return of calls
- Proper speaker phone usage
- Cooperative interaction with the firm's support services staff, legal assistants, and secretaries
- Placing only the client's file on the desk during a meeting with that client

- Ensuring the secretary will greet the client promptly in the reception area when you are delayed

§ 5.02(b) Economic Realities

A new lawyer also needs to gain a threshold understanding of economic realities imposed by firm and client. Some of the demands placed on you by supervising attorneys are influenced by your firm's response to external economics and the service expectations clients have of them. See, for example, §§ 4.06, 4.09 [Part I, Expectations Nos. 17, 20].

Become aware of the firm's philosophy and goals, its services and "products," client base and general market targets, and various pricing structures. Increasingly, firms develop and offer services in response to needs expressed by existing clients and to opportunities they have identified in market segments. That is, firms are focusing outward to identify and meet client needs rather than exclusively inward according to traditional delineations among substantive legal specialties. See the discussion in § 4.04 [Part I, Expectation No. 15: "Spot Related Problems"]. New lawyers can gain a practical sense of their firm's services by observing techniques used by its rainmakers and other client-oriented lawyers to attract and retain clients. For a discussion of steps you can take to prepare for a future client development role, see § 7.02 [Part II, Expectation No. 10: "Lay the Foundation for Business Development"].

It is worthwhile to become acquainted generally with your firm's organizational structure and management and to develop an awareness of economic realities of business operations. New lawyers become familiar immediately with those aspects of "economics" that directly impact their daily performance: "keeping time," recording time, recording client file expenses, and meeting deadlines. Absent inquiry, however, many remain unaware of other aspects of their firm's business operations: the concept of attorney utilization, work-in-progress, billing policies and procedures, collection time lags and procedures, impact of late time slips on cash flow, investment in the firm's new associates, training, technological resources and data bases, types of expenses that are recovered from clients, firm client development activities, etc. For example, a report that summarizes work-in-progress on a matter is an important financial management tool because it measures the time lag between performing the work and billing; firm management reviews this type of report to monitor timeliness of billings, billing value, productivity, investments in time, etc.

Also acquaint yourself with the role of your firm's legal assistants, accounting staff, word processing, messengers, data processing staff, file room clerks, and other support service personnel.

APPLYING THIS EXPECTATION TO YOUR RESPONSIBILITIES

Ensure that you meet your obligation to demonstrate professional conduct — by adhering to ethical responsibilities including: confidentiality, attorney-client privilege, identification of potential conflicts, supervision of nonlawyer assistants, advocacy principles, trial conduct, and legal etiquette.

Acquaint yourself with an overview of the economics of your firm's business — goals, client base, key services, pricing structures, basic principles of financial management, and so forth.

6

Skills Development: Avoiding Pitfalls from the Start

§ 6.01 EXPECTATION NO. 2: UNDERSTAND AND CLARIFY ASSIGNMENTS

"What is the point of the assignment? What does my supervising attorney want me to do?" Frequently, inexperienced associates do not know the answers to these questions; they do not understand what the supervising attorney really expects. Recently a new lawyer was observed in a firm library commenting to a colleague, "Well, here goes. . . . I hope, for my sake, this is what the partner wants. I'm really not sure what he has in mind." Amid head-shaking and expressions of low-level frustration, they continued to speak, surrounded by a pile of open reporters, highlighted copies of cases, and filled legal pad sheets — all of which, presumably, required a substantial amount of time to assemble and study and expense to reproduce.

What questions could this associate have asked to find out what the supervising attorney expected? Where do communication lapses frequently occur? Most new associates who were previously summer associates received assignments in carefully defined pieces. As new associates they will find their projects longer and less predictable in scope. This section addresses how to clarify an assignment received as a first year associate.

Supervising attorneys expect, first, that you have understood — or soon will understand, upon reviewing the file — the objective of the assignment, its due date, and other material specifications. If you do not, they expect you to ask questions and to fill in their lapses in instructions. Just as a supervising attorney must not commit the cardinal sin of assuming with a client, do not assume with a supervising attorney; he or she is your "client." In a very real sense, your supervising attorney is the first real client you will serve. Thus, do not automatically accept the sufficiency of the information that you have been given. Anticipate questions to which you need answers. Ask those questions to get essential specifications to clarify confusing instructions. Keep in mind, however, that you should defer some questions until you have consulted the file.

Supervising attorneys vary in the style in which they explain an assignment; even the same supervisor's approach and attention may vary, depending on what else is happening that day and how that associate presents himself. A supervising attorney who has had little contact with a junior associate may be unaware of the level of that associate's experience and may not have considered whether more or less direction will be needed. Another supervising attorney may simply not have the time to wait for questions. Still another knows the associate has been given too little direction — in a cryptic yellow note stuck onto the file that has been dropped on the chair or desk — but decides to wait for questions. In some cases the supervisor knows that the significance of an instruction will not become apparent until the associate begins the assignment and rereads his or her notes.

Just as good students take responsibility for their own educations by asking questions based upon material they are "taught," confident new associates take the initiative to ask essential questions after the supervising attorney presents an assignment. In this sense, associates must participate in their own "education." Temerity has little place, yet inexperienced associates are often afraid to admit they do not understand what is expected of them and are even more afraid to ask uninformed, inappropriate, or "stupid" questions. Others are so eager to get on with the assignment that they neglect to back up and think about what is being said. Worse, they make conscious or unconscious assumptions about what the supervising attorney wants them to do. Not surprisingly, a first year associate's lack of understanding about an assignment results in wasted time as misdirected hours are written down or off and completion of the assignment is delayed. Worse still, the associate's mental wanderings, temerity, and inadequate completion of the assignment seem to leave an indelible mark on the supervising attorney's memory.

If the supervisor's schedule does not permit essential questions at the time a project is assigned, ask the supervising attorney, or his or her secretary, when you can sit down to further discuss the assignment. Some supervisors respond more favorably and more promptly to a note or memorandum. By preparing a memorandum for the file — setting forth the issues you have been asked to resolve and outlining your approach — you create a "record" which allows the supervisor to think through the project again, to make changes in the assignment, and to correct any glaring misunderstanding of the tasks you've been asked to perform. Other supervisors are best understood through the grapevine. Intense or extremely busy types are often "unapproachable" because of pressures, deadlines, and emergencies about which you know nothing. This often creates an even less conducive environment for asking questions. Here, the secretary, other lawyers, or legal assistants can assist you. The point is not to gossip but to efficiently fill in gaps in their instructions and your understanding.

By breaking down a supervising attorney's ultimate expectation into specifications that are unlikely to be reflected in the file, a new lawyer can consistently anticipate and address those that require clarification. Specifications relevant to any assignment generally include:

- Purpose
- Major tasks and sequencing; immediate "To Do's"
- Work product
- Due date, priority level
- Interim reporting and review checkpoints
- Time estimate and limitations
- Budgetary instructions
- Special timekeeping, billing procedures
- Special handling procedures
- Sources for information, firm resources
- Authority to delegate to legal assistant
- Directed contact with client, staff, outside advisors

See Appendix D, Checklist of Assignment Ground Rules. Refer to it to trigger questions to clarify these specifications and to record instructions.

The lawyer in the library at the beginning of this section likely had little or no idea of what the purpose of the assignment was and even less as to the work product required. To better understand the specifications of an assignment, general features of each of these components are explored.

§ 6.01(a) Purpose of Assignment

As each assignment is explained, make sure the supervisor makes clear its purpose. Unless you have this compass with which to direct and recheck your efforts, your work product may not be of value. In addition, this may be your only opportunity to glimpse the overall plan and how your assignment fits into it. For example, the purpose of the assignment may be to educate a judge about the compelling strengths of your client's case by filing a motion for partial summary judgment on one claim for relief or, perhaps, on the lack of evidence to support punitive damages. The supervising attorney may even indicate that he does not expect to win on the motion because the judge will probably decide to hear the plaintiff's case first. Your work product may be a research memorandum, the motion and supporting brief itself, or the client's affidavit. Regardless, in this example the goal of educating the court begins to give shape to the assignment and research needed.

You can test or clarify your understanding of the assignment's purpose by restating it: "You want me to determine whether . . ." or, "Our objective is. . . . Is my understanding correct?" Or prepare a written outline of your approach to the project, beginning with the goal. In confirming the purpose of the assignment, you are translating "what is going on here" into "where are we going": the basis from which you determine what you are expected to do and what you are expected to produce.

§ 6.01(b) Major Tasks and Sequencing; Immediate Actions

You will have to determine the major tasks that must be performed; this will be the framework for your work plan. If you have not had this type of project before, or if it is more complex, you may be advised to review your understanding about the major tasks with the supervising attorney. This can be accomplished orally or by outlining the approach in writing. Note, however, that often you cannot expect to define the scope of an issue until you begin tackling the project. Also, identify those items that require immediate action. Following an assignment, take initial management steps:

Fill in notes
Review the file
Divide the assignment into manageable parts
Carry out immediate To Do's (*see* § 6.02(d)(1))
Assess lead time needed
Set a start date
Integrate it into your workload schedule
Develop a work plan

See §§ 6.02-6.03 [Part II, Expectation Nos. 3, 4].

§ 6.01(c) Work Product

The work product is what you will produce: it's what you will sign and submit to the supervising attorney, give to a client, or file with the court. Too often new lawyers ignore the importance of the culmination of their efforts: remember, your reputation will be shaped by what you do, say, and produce. Your work product will represent you. *Do not forget it.* To produce a useful work product, you need to know what is expected. The supervising attorney may want a formal memorandum stating the questions, short answers, facts, discussion, and conclusion; only the answer and copies of controlling cases; or a two-page analysis for presentation at a meeting. Regardless, you must find out what you are to produce. The supervising attorney expects to use your work product. If you do not produce it, or you produce it incorrectly or with an inappropriate level of formality, it cannot be used. See § 6.06 [Part II, Expectation No. 7: "Make Your Work Product Useful"].

To be useful, it must be clearly written, complete, responsive, appropriately organized, and timely. This is where new associates encounter a particularly common communication stumbling block. Supervisors use various "shorthands" to describe certain assignments or types of work products. When an instruction is expressed in a shorthand you have not heard before, or relates to a project in which you have not been involved, clarify what is meant. And ask around the firm about labels or terms for work products you do not understand. For example, an assigning attorney tells you, "Prepare a 'confirming letter,'" "work up the file," or "diary yourself up for a 30-day status report." Many of these shorthands are routinely used and encompass specific elements. Often there are forms for them. What does the assigning attorney expect in your preparation of the status report? Does he or she intend to send it to the client or to use it as an internal planning tool?

Another common impediment to useful work products is the "draft." New lawyers are often told to submit their work product "in draft." Do all the things you do to finish a product: proofreading, cite checks, thoughtful sentence structure and transitions. It should be your best effort: it's your name and it's your product.

§ 6.01(d) Due Date; Priority Level

As the assigned attorney, you must ascertain when a work product is due — whether imposed by the supervising attorney, client, court, or by the structure or momentum of negotiations or a transaction — and do what it takes to meet the deadline. Unless you know the deadline of each project, you will be unable to assign priorities and manage the assignment and workload effectively, sanely, and with a sense of your own competence and confidence. A directive to "get it to me as soon as you can" needs to be translated into a more specific time frame.

Often, a due date or the priority status of a project may appear to create a problem when assigned: it conflicts with priorities of other matters or it appears to require more time than is given or available. For a discussion of other problems in managing a workload *see* § 6.02 [Part II, Expectation No. 3: "Manage Your Workload"]. Take the initiative to solve the problem before concluding that it cannot be done. Determine if the due date is absolute or if part of the project can receive a later due date. If it is, determine if any competing projects, or parts of projects, have more flexible deadlines that can possibly be juggled. Can you divide the project that requires immediate attention into smaller tasks that you can accomplish in smaller blocks of time? Can you delegate some of the required tasks to your secretary or to a legal assistant if appropriate (and if you know how to do them yourself)? Also ask or find out whether someone else has handled a similar project and, if so, check whether that other file contains helpful forms, briefs, or memoranda.

To assess whether the due date is a problem and what can be done to alleviate it, you also need to know the realities of what it takes to get various types of work product out. Consider your time, secretarial time, word processing schedules and procedures, effective use of a personal computer, legal assistant time (if appropriate), internal resources, and courier service in rush hour traffic, not to mention express mail schedules, and an available telecopy line. For example, if you anticipate that your work product will run several pages and the word processing pool turnaround time that day is double the normal period because of a securities offering, then a review set for the next morning will create a problem for all concerned. In such a situation, if the due date is fixed, timely inform the supervisor or personnel manager, as appropriate, that you might need authorization for priority status or additional support staff to meet the deadline. If, however, you are unable to take on the assignment unless the due date for all or part of the project can be moved back, inform the supervising attorney immediately and explain why. A commercial transaction may fail if preparation of necessary documents is late.

§ 6.01(e) Interim Reporting and Review Checkpoints

Interim review and reporting expectations — communication checkpoints and routines — vary among supervising attorneys and from matter to matter. Some supervising attorneys want to be informed of progress and status informally — by notes, conversations in the hall, etc. Others want formal reports — in-house memoranda, or copies of letters sent and documents served. In either event, supervisors want to be kept up to speed.

For some projects, the supervising attorney wants a progress report after a number of hours, a specified period of time, or when a specified event occurs. Assigned attorneys are advised to clarify, if necessary, what extent or type of work product will be expected by that time. Ask "What do you expect?" Sometimes only periodic discussions are necessary. *See* § 6.05 [Part II, Expectation No. 6: "Communicate Progress and Status"].

Often an associate may want to request periodic assessments of progress and establish checkpoints as the assignment is made. In this situation, an associate might say, "I expect to finish the first part by Wednesday but will need to confer with you before proceeding with the second part because. . . . Will you be free to discuss this on Thursday morning?"

A supervising attorney may expect you to send a completed work product directly to the client without review. You obviously need to know this expectation so the completed document is not left on your desk — as you wonder why your supervisor has forgotten about it.

§ 6.01(f) Time Estimates and Limitations

As an assigned attorney, you must ensure that you understand the extent of effort the supervisor expects you to give an assignment. For a research assignment, the expected depth of research may range from "See if you can find anything on this to help us; spend a few hours on it. . . ." to "Do whatever it takes to get an answer." For some projects, the focus is whether the client wants a Cadillac or a Ford. *See* § 4.06 [Part I, Expectation No. 17: "Use Economic Sense"]. Sometimes, you can infer how long it should take from the supervisor's explanation of the assignment and other similar assignments you have completed. Often, however, you are well advised to confirm your estimate by asking the supervising attorney to assess how long the project should take (and any time constraints). This information can guard against "overlawyering" a transaction — that is, resolving all doubts at greater expense than the value the client places on the objective, or the supervising attorney places on the assignment. *See* § 4.06 [Part I, Expectation No. 17]. It may also reveal any misunderstandings of what a project entails. Finally, as the framework of awareness and experience grows, the associate develops judgment to determine the effort required in reaching a client's objective.

CONSIDER:

A client asks the supervising attorney to send a copy of the statute on sales tax. The client wants to determine whether the company must pay. The supervisor decides that he is comfortable sending the statute as requested, and asks an associate to mail a copy of the section to the client and to "let him know that it applies." The associate, who has done some work for this client and is generally familiar with the business, prepares a four-page analysis concluding that the client must pay the tax, and attaches it to the copy of the section. The supervising attorney fails to notice that the associate's time for the analysis is included in the client's bill. The client calls the supervising attorney to complain about the charge. The associate assumed that preparing an analysis was part of the job; this mistake and a subsequent "write-down" of time could have been avoided by clarifying that a telephone call or one-paragraph letter was expected rather than an analysis.

§ 6.01(g) Budgetary Instructions

More clients are requiring their lawyers to estimate fees and expenses during the engagement process, to develop a budget, and to confer when planning to incur certain expenditures or to exceed estimates. See §§ 2.05, 4.06, 4.09 [Part I, Expectation Nos. 4, 17, 20]. Therefore, when you are assigned a lengthy project, ask about any budgetary and expense instructions that affect your assignment.

§ 6.01(h) Special Timekeeping, Billing Procedures

A major adjustment from the academic study of law to the business and practice of law is keeping time accurately. In law school, students are unconcerned with keeping track of time spent on research and in preparing for class and examinations. Upon entering a firm and receiving time sheets, slips, or software timekeeping programs, new lawyers commonly regard them as an annoyance and a worrisome tool used to measure their performance rather than as a business necessity.

Recording time accurately serves several functions: (1) It forms a record and description of service for the client; (2) It satisfies a documentation requirement for professional liability coverage; (3) It provides a check against your To Do list; (4) It provides your supervisor with information to evaluate your work and progress, and provides other partners the sole exposure and source of information they have about your work; and (5) It provides management with attorney utilization and pricing data.

Record your time contemporaneously with each activity. If you wait until the end of the day and reconstruct tasks, you will have omissions. If you have recorded activities somewhere other than on the timesheet (for example, in a daily planner), transfer your notes to that day's time sheet by the close of the day. You are advised to set up a system with your secretary to promptly fill in mechanical data such as file numbers and to transmit the report.

It cannot be restated too often: record actual time. If you think a task should have taken less time, record actual time. To do otherwise is not your decision. You know neither the partner's thoughts on billing the client nor the impact on your evaluation. You can, however, write a note or cover memo to the supervising attorney explaining why a project took longer or was completed more quickly than expected. This information may help the supervising attorney determine how to appropriately bill the client and to assess the firm's investment in the matter. Remember that the billing attorney does not necessarily know everything you are doing on behalf of a client unless you communicate it.

Determine if there are special instructions for reporting time. In some situations, a supervising attorney may decide to deviate from the normal billing procedure or the client may have its own procedures which the firm has agreed to follow. When the client is billed a fixed fee for a matter, timekeeping is still important. To monitor the appropriateness of a fixed fee for a particular type of matter, the firm needs to track its investment in similar projects.

In describing how they have spent their time, new lawyers often neglect to consider the client's objective or perception of value, but instead focus on their supervising attorney's anticipated question: "What have you been doing?" In fact the supervising attorney expects each activity to be described in terms that are meaningful to the client. See §§ 3.02, 4.06 [Part I, Expectation Nos. 7, 17]. Various descriptions written by the supervising attorney serve as examples. Many firms use printed verb codes and activity codes on their daily time sheets to prompt appropriate descriptive language. For example, verb codes used by one firm in its litigation department include: "Analysis of," "Draft," "Interview," "Prepare for and attend," "Telephone conference with . . . regarding." Become aware of descriptions that many clients find annoying, such as "interoffice conference." Reference to the topic discussed may be preferable.

Finally, record your nonbillable categories of time. Many firms require it. Even if your firm does not, it is still important. Bar activities, pro bono work, CLE time, and participation in outside organizations let your supervising attorney and management know "what you have been doing." See §§ 7.01-7.02 [Part II, Expectation Nos. 9, 10].

§ 6.01(i) Special Handling Procedures

Some clients have developed special handling procedures which they expect the firm lawyers to follow. The procedures may be oral or written. For example, a client insurance company may have developed a form for status reports, may direct the lawyers to distribute copies of correspondence in duplicate to designated personnel, and may specify communication channels in various phases of litigation. If computer compatibility exists between the firm and the client, some procedures may involve electronic transmission of drafts for review. Some firms also create their own procedures for certain client matters. Corporate counsel often have a list of ground rules that they and the outside lead attorney agree upon during the engagement process. These rules may encompass division of responsibilities between inside counsel and the outside firm, roles of each individual who will work on the matter, guidelines or approval for hiring experts, a budget, reimburseable expenses, etc. See § 4.09 [Part I, Expectation No. 20].

§ 6.01(j) Sources of Information, Firm Resources

To effectively handle a project, assess whether information in addition to that in the file is necessary and how to obtain it. The assigning attorney may give you leads; the firm librarian or a legal assistant may have hands-on experience in efficiently investigating, locating, and obtaining factual nonlegal data through electronic databases, networking, printed materials, and governmental agencies.

Using outside sources and assistance reduces your control over timing. It also requires you to carefully plan to set realistic deadlines that allow for time to obtain and study the data, and to follow up. If you recognize the likelihood that you will need an outside resource at the time an assignment is explained and you are uncertain whether you are authorized to pursue it, discuss it with the supervising attorney. Early recognition avoids later delay in obtaining permission, if required, to proceed.

Find out where form files, research files, brief banks, and other internal work product files or precedent files for your practice are located. You may be able to find quality control or source manuals that compile opinion letters, lists of out-of-town court reporters used by firm members, credentials of experts, and form interrogatories and requests for production. Again, your firm's staff are good sources for locating firm resources. Other members of the firm can introduce you to computer capabilities to perform numerical analysis or to search documents in a litigation matter, to courier services, and to telecopier capability.

CONSIDER:

An investment banking firm assigns its outside lawyers to draft the documents for a transaction involving registration of debt securities. The investment banking firm's inside lawyers are using the outside firm because of caseload constraints. The investment banking firm has handled several similar transactions for this issuer. The associate assigned to draft the documents is unaware that the investment banking firm has handled similar transactions for the issuer, and has had no contact with the client investment banking firm. What questions do you ask?

What happened?

Because the supervising attorney and associate fail to discuss this client's previous agreements, the associate "reinvents the wheel," resulting in billable time that may be questioned by the supervising attorney, if not the client. Thus, a relatively inexpensive project has turned into a costly effort and the tone of this transaction is inconsistent with those between these parties in the past. A substantial portion of the associate's time devoted to the project must be written off.

§ 6.01(k) Authority to Delegate to Legal Assistant

As discussed in Part I, sophisticated clients, especially corporate counsel, often require notice or discussion with the lead attorney before additional lawyers or legal assistants are assigned to their respective matters. Some have guidelines or procedures they wish to have followed that may or may not be referred to in the fee or engagement letter.

During your first year, the supervising attorney may not want you to delegate in many situations. Supervising attorneys expect you to learn how to prepare such mundane work products as, for example, in the litigation department, a notice of deposition, a subpoena, and routine pleadings, and to learn the significance of alternative provisions. Therefore, before delegating tasks to a legal assistant, seek the supervising attorney's permission. Conversely, after you have learned these and other tasks, learn to delegate. Billing time for such tasks at mid-level associate hourly rates makes little "economic sense" to a client aware of the firm's resources (and little sense to the firm).

Generally, delegate tasks that allow you to use your time more efficiently. Delegable tasks may include a variety of tasks necessary to process facts: investigation, summarization, compilation, and document organization, computerization, and retrieval.

When you do delegate, explain precisely the delegated task, your objective, the result you expect the recipient of the task to achieve, and its place in the overall project (similar to the "flight plan" information you expect from your supervising attorney). Give the legal assistant enough information and authority to make intelligent decisions within the scope of the assignment. Include the legal assistant in the planning process as it relates to delegated tasks; this will help clarify the level of mutual understanding, reveal areas you may need to monitor more closely than others, and you will learn how the legal assistant can help leverage your time. This approach also creates interest and involvement in the project and helps the legal assistant to anticipate and plan for the workload demands of your matter. *See* Appendix G, Assignment Management Worksheet. Efficient and accurate performance more than offsets the initial expenditure of time needed to ensure the legal assistant understands your expectations. It is also advisable to direct the legal assistant to promptly prepare a memorandum of all conversations with outside contacts.

When delegating, do so with recognition of the ethical constraints on the use of a legal assistant: Understand that the lawyer is professionally and ethically fully responsible for the direct supervision of work assigned — that is, the lawyer is responsible for what legal assistants do. *See* ABA Model Rule 5.3. Also recognize that there may be some tasks a legal assistant is not expected to do. A firm may assign someone other than a legal assistant to perform specific functions such as, for example, serving process or checking court records in another county. Unless work which is secretarial is part of a legal assistant's job with the firm, do not assign such work to him or her; confer with the legal assistant administrator or personnel manager on those tasks. Otherwise, the client might be billed for secretarial services at the legal assistant's rate. For guidelines in delegating to your secretary and establishing a good working relationship, *see* § 6.03 [Part II, Expectation No. 4: "Manage Your Assignments"].

§ 6.01(l) Directed Contact with Client, Staff, Outside Advisors

As an assignment is given, determine whether (and to what extent) the supervising attorney expects you to contact the client, its staff, or the client's outside advisor to obtain further information, to relay information, to discuss alternatives and answer questions, etc. Exclusive contact may remain with the supervising attorney for one or more reasons. If, however, you are expected to interact with the client contact or other advisor, it is important that the supervising attorney define your role and responsibilities. Also ask whether the client knows you will be involved in the matter so you can plan a smooth introduction. Firms lose clients because of poorly orchestrated delegations and supervision. Clients have mentioned their annoyance and confusion or questions as to management of their cases when unintroduced lawyers contact them and unfamiliar names show up on the signature lines of letters. Here, a little communication and consideration go a long way.

It is also important to clarify the limits of your authority to make decisions commensurate with the responsibility assigned to you.

CONSIDER:

For example, your assignment is to prepare the responses to plaintiff's interrogatories. Some of the interrogatories request information, some of which may be sensitive and concern the client's cost of doing business.

- Are you authorized to call the client or are you expected to relay your questions through the supervising attorney?
- Will your first communication with the client be a letter forwarding unobjectionable interrogatories and requesting responses and comments?
- Will the letter go out under your signature or the supervising attorney's signature?

CONSIDER:

You are asked to send the draft of the contract you prepared to the client for "review." A few days later, the supervising attorney asks if the client suggested changes or had questions. You are surprised and respond, "I haven't spoken with him." It is up to you to find out whether you are expected to call the client to follow up or whether the supervising attorney intends to do so.

If a fee or engagement letter is available to you, its terms may cover several areas that provide a context for your assignment. *See* §§ 2.05, 2.07, 4.06 [Part I, Expectations Nos. 4, 6, 17]. You will find reference to a well-drafted fee letter invaluable as you work through a matter; it is a tool by which you monitor adherence to the terms agreed upon. The new matter client intake sheet may also contain instructive data.

APPLYING THIS EXPECTATION TO YOUR RESPONSIBILITIES

Find out the objective of your assignment.

Anticipate and clarify material specifications that are unlikely to be addressed in the file:

- Work product expected.
- Major tasks and sequencing; immediate To Do's.
- Due date, priority level.
- Interim reporting and review checkpoints.
- Time estimates and limitations.
- Budgetary instructions.
- Special timekeeping, billing procedures.
- Special handling procedures.

Sources for information, firm resources.

Authority to delegate to legal assistant.

Directed contact with client or staff, outside advisors.

---

§ 6.02 EXPECTATION NO. 3: MANAGE YOUR WORKLOAD AND TIME

Supervising attorneys expect new associates to manage assignments in a logical, timely, and efficient manner. They often presume that new lawyers have created a workable method of their own, even though they have had little or no experience juggling competing assignments, and managing a caseload. New lawyers soon realize that the value, character, and relative importance of projects frequently change. In fact, the frustration expressed most often by first year associates is that they are unprepared to manage their workloads.

A common misconception among recent graduates is that they can mentally schedule and retain everything they need to do for all of their assignments. This approach is often maintained until the first assignment is overlooked or the first deadline is missed. Why do we believe we can remember everything? Because in the past, we have, or we've come very close.

During law school a student is single-purposed, following a linear progression from assignment to assignment, preparing for the mid-term and final examinations. Classes are held at the same hour each week and the examinations are scheduled — to the day and hour — well in advance. There are no chances of the exam being "bumped," "continued," or "rescheduled," because of an emergency negotiation or meeting. (For many courses, previously administered examinations are on file that effectively guide the student in determining what is necessary to meet the expectations of the "client.")

Summer associate programs and law school clinical programs, although tremendously valuable for some things, do not exist to teach an associate caseload management. Instead, the summer programs' primary focus is to evaluate summer associates and to market the firm to desired recruits. Assignments are given in bite-size chunks of short duration. The supervising attorney and recruitment coordinator check on them frequently.

In stark contrast are the daily shifts in scheduling and time demands in the practice of law. A trying aspect of practice, regardless of specialty or type, is that everything on your calendar can change with a phone call. Literally everything.

New lawyers, although initially lacking an effective management style and many self-organization skills, must quickly learn to manage a fluid, shifting workload. Workload management, in turn, becomes the cornerstone of a style of practice in which good judgment can be developed and exercised regularly, and excellent client service can be delivered — a "workstyle." Some of the recurring problems and obstacles that new lawyers face can often be resolved by managing a workload and assignments. Self-generated obstacles arise if components of workload management are neglected, including:

Clarifying Due Date, Priority Status Among Projects

Estimating Time Required for a Matter, Task

Knowing the Status of Active Matters at a Glance

Reassigning Priorities

Recording Deadlines and Reminders

Managing Time

Scheduling Tasks on Daily, Weekly To Do List

Working Effectively with a Secretary

Managing Assignments

In § 6.01 [Part II, Expectation No. 2: "Understand and Clarify Assignments"], initial inquiries were outlined to clarify the due date and priority level of a project or its segments, and to estimate time expected spent on an assignment. The other components are addressed in this Expectation and in Expectation No. 4: "Manage Your Assignments."

§ 6.02(a) Know the Status of Active Matters at a Glance

To assist in managing an active workload, consider keeping a case-flow chart that lists the due date, priority ranking and major tasks for each active matter. A chart works because it provides a current "snapshot" of your active caseload. At a glance you can use the chart to anticipate demands among competing matters, to prepare a weekly and daily To Do list (discussed in § 6.02(d)(1)), to recognize the need from time to time to affirm and reassign relative priorities among projects and to juggle projects as priorities shift. If a project abruptly demands most of your attention, reference to the chart will prompt you to quickly assess the impact on other assignments. The chart also serves as a reminder for the small percentage of files you do not like or want to tackle, but must. Figure 6.1 contains a sample case-flow chart. *See also* Appendix E.

This chart is prepared and updated from instructions and the assignment work plan discussed in Expectation No. 4: "Manage Your Assignments." Under each major task you list, it is advisable to enter your estimated starting and completion dates.

The chart helps you organize and gives you perspective on your caseload. Priority ranking among projects is not necessarily the same as the order of their due dates. One may require earlier attention than another that is due first. If, after taking immediate action, nothing further must be done for a while, that project's priority level would be adjusted to reflect the time when work should be resumed.

FIGURE 6.1: CASE FLOW CHART

Updated: ______________________

Matter	Assignment Date	Priority Rank	Major Task	Major Task	Major Task	Date Due
			Start: Complete:	Start: Complete:	Start: Complete:	
			Start: Complete:	Start: Complete:	Start: Complete:	
			Start: Complete:	Start: Complete:	Start: Complete:	
			Start: Complete:	Start: Complete:	Start: Complete:	

§ 6.02(b) Reassign Priorities Among Matters and Tasks

To manage your workload as several matters compete for your attention, you must not only determine the priority of each assignment when you receive it but periodically reassess it thereafter.

Priority status of a matter may change for many reasons, including unfolding complexity, a change in the client's circumstances, or a change in the tempo of a case. Variables that determine the relative priority of a matter include:

- Due date
- Flexibility in extending due date: time, cost, strategy
- Change in client's circumstances and priorities
- Lead time needed to carry out tasks; complexity
- Control over allocation and scheduling of firm or outside resources
- Flexibility in scheduling work on current phase of other projects

Assessing and adjusting priorities presupposes effective management of individual assignments. Assignment management is discussed below in Expectation No. 4; guidelines and checkpoints for communicating progress and status of an assignment to the supervising attorney are addressed in Expectation No. 6.

By assigning and reassigning relative priorities to each of your projects, you will maintain perspective — a critical element of "workstyle."

When you find yourself inundated with projects you cannot put in order, or establish priorities for — let alone complete — inform your supervising attorneys and enlist their aid in saying "no" to any additional projects. Then seek their assistance in assigning priorities. Consider, for example, this associate's response to a memo assigning a "short fused" task: "To pull those numbers together on *Wilson* by tomorrow I'll have to defer evaluating the *Lane* situation you assigned yesterday. Unless I hear otherwise, I'll work on *Wilson* first and get back to *Lane* next." If two or more supervising attorneys have given you conflicting matters and you are unable to resolve the conflicts yourself, ask who has first call on your time instead of making speculative decisions yourself or informing that you cannot get to the assignment a few hours before it is due. If you are assigned a mentor, or assignment coordinator, seek his or her advice. Do not simply disregard a due date you find arbitrary. By doing so, you may be considered undependable or unfairly accused of exercising poor judgment, regardless of your undisclosed rationale.

§ 6.02(c) Record Deadlines

Most new lawyers soon realize the imperative of calendaring scheduled appointments and events through their secretaries and using the firm's or department's docket control system to avoid missing conferences, and obvious deadlines such as court dates, statutes of limitations, closings, and due dates governing the other side. If, for example, opposing counsel does not respond to your interrogatories or request for production and, having failed to record a reminder date, you neglect to file a motion to compel a response, then a judge might not issue sanctions later if you claim "surprise" to their documents or witnesses that you sought to be identified in the interrogatories. Ensure that your system also picks up subtle deadlines, such as conference calls, follow-ups for inactive matters, a date when action on a project must begin, the deadline to designate an expert witness, and expected response dates set out in correspondence. Also record the dates you give the client by which to furnish information. A client or outside advisor may be a "two week man" unless prodded periodically. For those who have a personal computer in their offices, also consider software packages that have calendar entries. Some have formulas that facilitate setting related dates, deadlines, and reminders — for example, form filing or statute dates. *Do not only calendar: react to the calendar.*

Carry a pocket calendar or a daily planner in your briefcase. When you are away from the office and schedule a meeting, telephone appointment, or other activity, enter it. Upon returning to the office, tell your secretary each of the events that you have scheduled and all deadlines you set or received.

Some new lawyers neglect to consistently report scheduling information to their secretaries or decide it is too important to share with the secretary — that's backwards! In the final analysis it is *your* responsibility if you miss a deadline or a meeting. If your calendar, the docket control system, and your secretary have incomplete information, none is a reliable primary source or a backup. Your secretary is there to help you. Enlist the help and the resources of your secretary to ensure that you will not miss a deadline. See § 6.02(e) below, "Work Effectively with Your Secretary."

§ 6.02(d) Manage Your Time

Do you careen from crisis to crisis, muttering around the office or fretting constantly over your many tasks, and accomplishing few? If so, you probably do not follow an internal process that positions you, your secretary, or legal assistant, so that you can each exercise good judgment and then act successfully, instead of reacting to hurriedly assessed alternatives. Cumulative judgments in recurring crises do not represent your best work. If preventable crises fill your days and you cannot be bothered to change, here is a glimpse of your likely future: burnout, extreme stress, supervising attorney and client dissatisfaction, self-dissatisfaction, and worse.

§ 6.02(d)(1) To Do List

Prepare a daily and weekly "To Do" list of tasks for all matters from the work plan and checklists you've prepared for each assignment or case, your calendar, and docket control system. *See* § 2.05 [Part II, Expectation No. 4: "Manage Your Assignment"]. *See* Appendix F for a sample To Do list to use in conjunction with a daily planner. There are also software packages available in which you can make entries for tasks, appointments, and tickler reminders to warn of approaching deadlines or events. The To Do list cuts across all projects so that you can orchestrate progress in each. It only takes a few minutes to prepare a To Do list. Do this as the last item of business each day and week or as the first task each morning and week.

Assign priorities to each of the activities as they are inserted on the To Do list for that day to accomplish your goals: "A" for urgent, scheduled, must do; "B" for important, do if possible; and "C" for optional items. The point is to focus attention to activities in sufficient time to exercise good judgment and produce interim results geared toward achieving the client's objective. Unavoidably, part of each day is unpredictable. In scheduling tasks, anticipate that part of each day will not be available. The "stacks-of-files-on-the-desk-or-floor" (or in-basket directed) method to determine daily activities and to remind of cases that need attention consumes much more time as files are reordered and checked. More significantly, you may well overlook a file that is removed from your office or lost among larger files. Reacting to those files within arm's reach does not work for long.

Consistently following a well-intentioned To Do list presupposes exercise of time management skills. From the time management seminars, articles, and books that abound, the following thoughts and suggestions may help make your To Do lists work. First, get some perspective on how you currently manage work. Record each of today's activities chronologically. If today becomes both "crazy" and unusual, then also record tomorrow's activities. (If, instead, you were to reconstruct yesterday's activities as data for this analysis, you would probably fail to recall wasted time.) Mark those activities which were "A," "B," and "C" levels — and those which fall below "C" level. "A" activities result from:

1. Planning — scheduled meetings, conference calls, returning calls — they are on the To Do list
2. Unavoidable crises — those which could not be foreseen and defused
3. Procrastination and poor planning

If you reduce procrastination, you create time to address the "B's," which accumulate and desperately demand a flurry of actions. Although the first type of "A" situations is generally positive, beware of overbooking yourself, thereby precluding attention to "B" activities that necessarily require some designated portion of your time each day.

Poor time managers find they list many "A" and "C" level activities, but have not fired a shot on "B" activities. "B's" require planning and active project management to appear on the To Do list. Frequently, there simply is not time for "B" activities — they are not crises, they do not litter the in-basket, and they do not intrude as incoming calls or unannounced visitors.

Occasionally an ignored "B" level task can later create a disaster. For example, a lawyer's failure to follow up with the expert witness to discuss that expert's report before the pretrial order was due. Here is another example of a "B" activity that is often neglected until it becomes an "A" level crisis. You receive an assignment for which you believe or are told there is a "form that just needs to be customized a little." As it turns out, the form requires significant changes and the project itself demands hours of research. It cannot be overemphasized — "B's" are too often left to smolder until they become real fires.

"C" level activities also have their place, sometimes as a necessary mental break from urgent or intense work. They need careful management, however, to keep them in perspective: they often appear, mistakenly, to require less time to begin or complete than expected, or they are delegable with appropriate supervision. If work on "C" tasks begins too early during the day, you may run out of time to properly handle "A" and "B" tasks.

§ 6.02(d)(2) Some Suggestions

1. Decide on the next step or disposition while reading the contents of the in-basket or surveying a new file. Do not merely transfer papers to another location in the office — credenza, table, drawer, or floor. Put them in the out-basket with an instruction and make a note on the To Do list, a checklist, or calendar and docket system, as appropriate.

2. Carefully consider whether some "C" activities on your To Do list can be delegated to your secretary or to a legal assistant.

3. Tackle the "A" level projects at the time of the day you work best — begin them earlier rather than later to ensure you get them all accomplished.

4. Become aware of practices that waste your time and determine how they can be corrected. For example, be alert to time wasted by disorganization such as leaving tasks unfinished that should be completed while you are focused on the project, a poor filing system, socializing, or unclear communication between you and your secretary or you and the supervising attorney.

5. Designate a reasonable period of time (very early, very late) each day to work without *routine* interruptions. Also inform your secretary of your priorities and set up an internal system so nonemergency calls are held during that period, in-basket material is not delivered, and peers do not drop in. If you consistently return calls promptly, nonemergency callers will have

confidence that you will get back to them shortly and will be less likely to insist on "catching" you now.

6. Think broadly about completing the entire project. Ask yourself for each task listed: could this be done in a better, more efficient way? Note the reminders you will have to give others to avoid a last minute crisis.

7. For a new project on which work must begin, create the beginning of a work plan and list a specific task instead of "start working on Smith file." It is much easier to put off beginning work on a matter that appears overwhelming than to avoid tackling a definite task.

8. End telephone conversations that become social firmly but graciously so you can get on with your work. Do not be afraid to close the call with a commitment to phone back at a specified time and date to continue the conversation.

9. Check your To Do list priorities against the "big picture" priorities listed on the case flow chart.

10. List things you need to do on a case as soon as you think of them. If you do not make a note of them right away, you may forget them by the time it is convenient to write them down. Then transfer them to the project's checklist.

§ 6.02(e) Work Effectively with Your Secretary

To manage assignments effectively and efficiently presupposes a good working relationship between new associate and secretary. More than an occasional second year associate has sighed, "I am grateful to receive a secretarial reassignment – now I can start over. I did not know how to work with my secretary and it was a disaster." Building mutual trust and working as a team instead of functioning as two uncoordinated individuals requires effort and commitment. You and your secretary share common goals of delivering client service, achieving job satisfaction,and gaining respect of colleagues. The following are some suggestions to get off to a good start.

Many firms have created a procedures manual or issued instructional memoranda that address secretarial responsibilities and administrative policies. Acquaint yourself with procedures that impact on your work and expectations. Find out, for example, the division of typing responsibilities between secretaries and word processing staff; a secretary may be expected to type documents or letters of less than five pages. Also become aware of the circumstances in which secretarial and word processing time are billed to clients. To use support services and resources efficiently, acquaint yourself with procedures for telecopy requests, messenger pick-up or delivery, express mail, equipment check-out, print shop projects, library and file-room check-out procedures, and so forth.

Your firm may have a policy on answering telephone calls. More firms now pass calls from the switchboard directly to lawyers' offices instead of screening calls; some encourage attorneys to give their direct dial numbers and expect them to place their own calls. Familiarize yourself with policies and procedures such as message center or voice mail instructions.

Focus on defining and communicating your initial expectations of your secretary. Discuss, for example, your respective responsibilities in scheduling and maintaining the calendar, filling out docket system entry slips, and procedures for in-basket and out-basket paperwork flow. You will develop additional expectations as the variety and complexity of assignments increase and as you become familiar and comfortable with your secretary's capabilities. Your secretary can also offer practical advice or help you with administrative procedures, for example in arranging for service of process with the outside process service.

The secretary is a vital contact point and communication link from the client to the attorney. Inform your secretary when you are leaving the floor or the office, where you are going, when you expect to return, and whether to forward calls if you are in the library. Determine how you want your secretary to take telephone messages. What is a good message that will save you time and convey to callers your accessibility and interest in their matters? Also observe how the secretary takes messages for a senior attorney. Let the secretary know who you expect may call and what to say if the call comes in. Clearly relate questions you want the secretary to ask or information you want to obtain.

Ensure that the secretary is aware that the attorney-client privilege extends to information clients convey to her on your behalf so that she can explain this, as appropriate. If you want a call routed to someone else in your absence, or a telephone appointment scheduled if certain persons should call, let your secretary know that.

If you have a personal computer in your office, discuss and establish work flow procedures that maximize efficient production of work product. The goal is to provide cost-effective service to the client. You may determine that you draft a document more skillfully using the computer than dictating it but edit from hard copy. Make sure you communicate your expectations and preferences to the secretary.

Periodically discuss, "What's working?" "What needs improvement?" "How can we work together better?" Finally, ask yourself, "If I were my secretary, would I be happy working with me?"

For a discussion of delegation to your secretary, see § 5.05(b)(3) [Part II, Expectation No. 4: "Manage Your Assignments"].

APPLYING THIS EXPECTATION TO YOUR RESPONSIBILITIES

Components of Integrating a Matter into Your Workload and Managing Your Workload Include:

Knowing the status of each active matter at a glance

Reassessing and reassigning priorities as variables change: due dates and flexibility in scheduling work among projects; changes in client's circumstances and priorities; momentum; lead time needed to carry out a task; resources

Recording deadlines, tasks and reminders: use your secretary, calendar, and docket control system

Managing time through scheduling tasks on a "To Do" list and careful setting of priorities: A — urgent, B — important, C — optional

Working effectively with your secretary by defining and communicating your expectations; establishing responsibilities and procedures — Discuss periodically what is working, what is not, and how to work better together

---

§ 6.03 EXPECTATION NO. 4: MANAGE YOUR ASSIGNMENTS

Lawyers work for *results!* They seek the best outcome for their clients. Supervising attorneys expect attorneys to whom they delegate assignments to produce a useful work product. Managing the assignment is a prerequisite to producing a useful work product.

When you receive a new assignment, even though you are busy, to manage you must work it into your workload as soon as possible.

§ 6.03(a) The First Step

The following are suggested routine procedures to follow when an assignment is received:

- Fill in assignment notes
- Incorporate immediate action items into the daily To Do list
- If none, review the file to realistically assess when work should begin to meet deadlines
- Integrate the assignment timeline and due date into your workload

§ 6.03(b) Create a Work Plan

Make a work plan. Just as gaining the summit of the mountain requires climbing to the ridge first, accomplishing the result a client seeks requires planning to complete interim steps aimed at the objective. How each step is taken and completed may well determine the final outcome. As good trial lawyers know, "Good on your feet at trial" results from good preparation at your desk.

As you create a work plan of the steps you will take, you must make a series of professional judgments. Clients want and expect the lawyer's professional judgment to help them make decisions relating to operations, planning, or dispute resolution. Supervising attorneys observe your judgments to decide if you are ready for advanced assignments and increased client contact. Thus, your success depends on ensuring that your plans, judgments, and management translate into the best incremental service and results you can provide. Your focus on the ultimate "result" should not obscure the importance of planning and achieving interim results. Planning and managing an assignment benefits the client and the lawyer because it:

- Focuses and maintains a lawyer's attention on the client's objective and expectation of consistent service. (In fact, the originating attorney probably emphasized superior service and work product in attracting the client.)
- Fosters an organized, thoughtful environment in which the lawyer can better pace work and exercise good judgment. The lawyer can also make better time and cost estimates for future assignments.

CONSIDER:

You are instructed to meet with a client and opposing counsel to persuade opposing counsel not to file suit against the client because it is without merit. You determine what you have to do to prepare for the meeting and check whether the documentation in support of your client's position is in the file. It is not. The next step is to call the client, if authorized, or your supervising attorney, to request the documentation for your review before the meeting. If you had not checked the file and made the call *sooner* rather than later, the client (or supervising attorney) might be out of town or otherwise unable to gather the information in time for you to prepare.

The all-too-common consequences of failing to plan ahead can be illustrated with a situation analogous to solving the typical legal problem: the assembly of a child's gift from Santa. At about one in the morning you discover that the cotter pin needed to hold the steering wheel of that shiny four-foot-long fire engine is not in the bag of parts. This disaster, a fire engine that does not work Christmas morning, would not have happened if only you had checked the instructions and parts list the day before. As your child looks to you questioning the existence of Santa, so will your client, questioning the existence of your competence and judgment. The client, for example, expected to use the proceeds of the sale you are handling to meet an obligation due on the day of closing, and you forgot to check to see if the contract called for payment in immediately available funds.

§ 6.03(b)(1) Break Projects into Manageable Parts

To create a work plan divide a large assignment into subprojects or a smaller project directly into major tasks. Outline the plan. If the assignment is complex, it may be helpful to diagram that sequence with a flow diagram. By enabling you to see the project as a whole and the relationships among major tasks, a flow diagram forms a framework for planning and pacing your work. This tool prompts you to anticipate which tasks require more lead time than others and to anticipate additional tasks that are likely to lie a step-and-one-half ahead of the immediate scope of the assignment. *See* Appendix G, Assignment Management Worksheet. As work is performed, you can readjust your plan and add to your flow diagram the tasks of exploring, assessing, and testing "what if" alternatives; in essence, part of your diagram can become a decision tree. The need to update the supervising attorney on your progress or seek guidance may become apparent. *See* § 6.05 [Part II, Expectation No. 6: "Communicate Progress and Status"]. For those of you who have access to a personal computer, there are numerous project outlining and management software packages available. *See* Figure 6.2 for a sample assignment flow diagram.

When you find yourself overwhelmed by a new assignment look for any immediate To Do's. If none are apparent, tackle it by focusing on its overall objective and allocating a small block of time in which to make a start. Use that time to review the file, isolate research that appears to be central to the project, identify information you need to collect, or list persons who you believe you will need to contact and the purposes for the contacts. Then define and outline the major tasks

FIGURE 6.2: SAMPLE ASSIGNMENT FLOW DIAGRAM

Assignment objective: ______________________________

Work Product expected: ______________________________

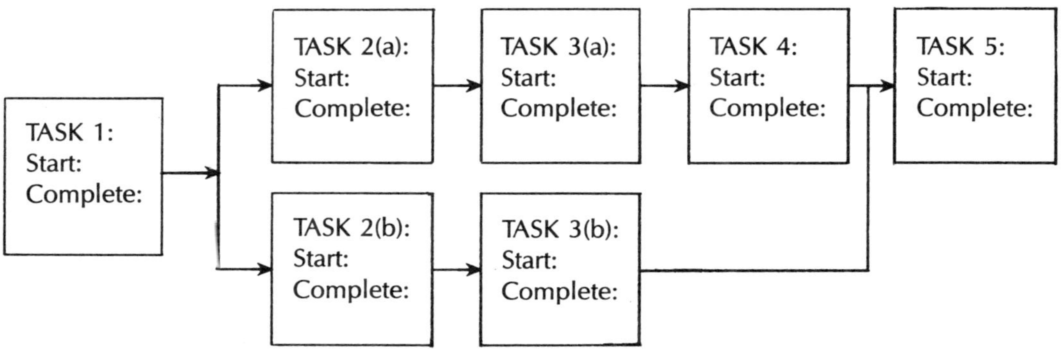

and sequencing, refining and reassessing them as you dig into the assignment.

§ 6.03(b)(2) *Construct Timetable and Budget Time*

Budgeting time among tasks and constructing a timetable imposes discipline and sets a self-pacing structure for the assignment. This step also facilitates appropriate allocation of time among competing projects and timely entry on the To Do lists.

Anticipate the time needed to carry out each major task – optimal, probable, and worst case – within the prescribed time period for the project. Moving from the assignment due date or date promised back to the assignment date, construct a timeline by designating start and completion dates for each subproject or task. If it is up to you to set the assignment due date, start with the date it was received and move forward to budget time and set a reasonable completion date. Insert the time estimates onto the outline or diagram. Also enter the two or three major tasks and dates on the workload case flow chart. *See* Appendix E.

For time estimates to serve as an effective tool for managing work flow toward the final deadline, or complying with budgetary or billable time constraints, the estimates must be realistic. If, for example, the work product will go to the client for review and comments, extra time must be allotted for that purpose. Similarly, additional time must be allotted if the supervising attorney expects to integrate your work product into his.

As you prepare the timeline, consider reasons for actual and apparent unreasonable delays you have experienced on other matters. If you are able to isolate recurring causal patterns, you can often eliminate repetition of the problem when planning a new assignment. Many new lawyers fail to estimate lead time needed to begin or complete a task. For example, you began a task late and the outside resources you needed were unable to drop everything else or reorder their commitments to accommodate you immediately. Or, you failed to consider lead time needed in dealing with a government agency. Or, you were late in starting research because the due date appeared so far away, and you had not even looked at the file shortly after receiving the assignment to assess what would be involved. (You probably made an unfounded assumption.)

Working through an assignment work plan and timeline will reduce the potential for procrastination because the effect of procrastination becomes so apparent. While concentrating on other matters, the need to interrupt them to handle a task is readily determined. You will also become alerted to whether you need to reallocate or seek additional resources to complete the assignment on time.

§ 6.03(b)(3) Create Checklists

For each task that you have listed, construct a checklist of activities: substantive, administrative, and procedural. Note any sources consulted for information. Some activities in a checklist may be dictated by the outcome of earlier steps. As checklists are the product of organization, they also prompt better descriptions of time for billing purposes. After preparing a checklist of activities for a task, reassess the time budgeted for the task.

§ 6.03(b)(4) Delegate Appropriate Tasks

Delegating tasks effectively requires that the lawyer plan, set priorities, and communicate expectations. It also necessitates awareness of the secretary's workload and schedule among matters and attorneys, and daily priorities placed upon both of you by the firm, such as completing timesheets.

As a general guideline in determining what to delegate, identify tasks that your secretary can competently perform more efficiently or equally efficiently as you. Use of your checklists or flow diagram may be helpful in determining which tasks and minor decision-making activities recur frequently and can be cost-effectively delegated. Where possible assign a whole task instead of a piece, to avoid unnecessary coordination steps. By consistently receiving similar tasks, the secretary can become proficient in carrying them out. It is important, however, to balance delegation with self-training: do not delegate tasks that you are confused about; your expectations and directions will be unclear.

Define and clearly communicate the purpose of the task, what you expect to be achieved, time constraints, and relative priority of the task. Determine the extent of discretion the secretary will need to make decisions and to take actions in carrying out the task. Gradually, consider delegating some tasks that you perform more efficiently than your secretary. Those tasks should be introduced in bite-sized chunks and progress supervised accordingly.

Keep in mind these common sense "don'ts" of effective delegation: Don't assign a task and then do it yourself. Don't hover and second guess each step of your secretary's process in carrying out an assigned task. That approach swiftly conveys lack of trust. If you are concerned that the task has not been started, consider whether you clearly communicated the deadline, priority, expected effort needed, or checkpoints. Don't create unnecessary last minute pressure on your secretary by neglecting to organize yourself. Some lawyers assume they know how long a task will take their secretary to perform even though they have never asked or discussed it. Such speculation often results in a severe underestimate of what it takes to get the work product out.

Next, recognize what happens if a lawyer delegates similar tasks on an inconsistent basis, sporadically performing those tasks himself or herself. The secretary will probably become confused about that lawyer's expectations and conclude that she is not responsible for the assignments and need not worry because the lawyer will redo or complete them. This attitude yields inconsistent performance; the lawyer is left with little confidence that the secretary will predictably proceed from point A to point B. Finally, delegate credit but not blame. Some new lawyers make disparaging comments about a secretary's failure to carry out assignments and attempt to disassociate themselves from mistakes. They neglect to recognize that such behavior marks them as immature and unwilling to accept responsibility.

In some situations, the client as well as the supervising attorney must approve the assignment of a legal assistant to a project. When delegating to legal assistants, involve yourself with them in planning their tasks. Do not, however, use delegation to "dump" tasks that you do not know how to perform (hoping the delegatee will figure out what to do without recognizing, exposing, or compounding your confusion.) Do not, for example, delegate preparation of a *subpoena duces tecum* or a citation until you understand the relative significance of various procedures or language. For a discussion of delegation to a legal assistant, *see* § 6.01(k) "Authority to Delegate to Legal Assistant."

§ 6.03(b)(5) Enter Tasks onto To Do Lists

Checklist items from each matter should be entered onto the daily or weekly To Do lists, as appropriate. *See* § 6.02 [Part II, Expectation No. 3: "Manage Your Workload"] and Appendix F. Checklists for each project are not a substitute for a To Do list. The To Do list schedules tasks across the workload. As discussed earlier, assign priorities to each activity when inserting it onto the To Do list for that day and week: "A" for urgent, must do; "B" for important, do if possible; and "C" for optional items.

§ 6.03(b)(6) Illustrations

The following work plans illustrate a relatively straightforward matter – updating corporate minutes – and two more complex matters – an assignment to determine advice on health care coverage requirements, and a supplemental retirement plan.

A. Updating Corporate Minutes. You find a file on your desk with a note saying the supervising attorney wants you to update G Corporation's minutes. You have not worked on any G Corporation matters and are unfamiliar with the company beyond what is in the file. You ask the supervising attorney's secretary when the supervising attorney wants the minutes completed. The secretary does not know but agrees to find out for you. Before hearing anything, you check again the next morning and learn that there is a board meeting two weeks from tomorrow and that the minutes must be delivered to the client the day before the meeting. You examine the file and note that there is little helpful information to assess how much happened during the year. You leave the supervisor a note stating that you intend to contact the chief financial officer and the executive vice president to get the information needed, and that you want to enlist a legal assistant's help. After clearing this planned course of action, you prepare a list of topics, questions, and documents to ask these corporate officers, including: the names of current officers, shareholders, and directors; dates and decisions reached at the annual shareholders and board meetings; and, what major decisions and events have occurred during the year.

After selecting a format for the minutes, you explain to the legal assistant how the information should be applied to the format. Then you set a due date five days before the minutes must be delivered to the client to give you and the supervising attorney time to review the document. During one of your conversations, the chief financial officer raises a problem which may provide the firm with an opportunity to render additional service. You mention this possibility in a note to the supervising attorney that you attach to the minutes. *See* § 4.04 [Part I, Expectation No. 15: "Spot Related Problems"]. The supervising attorney makes a couple of comments in the margins of the minutes and you revise them. The supervising attorney delivers them to the client as they meet to prepare the client regarding some issues for the board meeting.

COMMENT:

This associate wisely took the time to look over the file in advance to plan for the lead time needed to gather the information, prepare the minutes, and submit the document for review by the supervising attorney.

B. Health Care Coverage Assignment. Suppose that the associate has the following instructions for a new project:

1. Determine specifically what the client company must do to comply with a new health care act — what coverage must be added or changed;
2. Submit a memorandum for review in four days.

The health plan is not in the file; because time is short, the associate requests the plan and arranges to have it picked up instead of mailed. Later that day the associate decides to become generally familiar with the requirements in the Act to determine how much research will be involved. Some of the coverage requirements appear straightforward, such as eligibility for continuous coverage. However, the definition of the new benefits the company must offer and the amount the company can charge will require further research. The associate realizes that some time will be needed to call the company to learn about how its administration might apply the new benefits and cost provisions. The checklist for the work plan looks like this:

1. (a) Conduct preliminary research.
   (b) Obtain health insurance plan.

2. (a) Examine plan and research specific requirements.

   (b) Make calls to client, as needed.

3. Draft memorandum.

4. Submit memorandum for review.

The day the plan arrives, the associate analyzes the additional coverage the client must offer, and determines the formula to discuss with the company to enable a more specific response. For an illustration of a memorandum's "deductively ordered summary" prepared for the client *see* § 6.06 [Part II, Expectation No. 7: "Make Your Work Product Useful"].

C. Supplemental Retirement Plan. On November 8th, the supervising attorney assigns an associate to draft a nonqualified supplemental retirement plan for the client company's top 25 executives out of 400 total employees. The firm has represented the client previously; some information is in the files, but the associate will have to develop most of the specifications and supporting information for the plan. In demonstrating the process, the associate's questions about the scope of the assignment and the supervising attorney's responses are included:

"Should I prepare a fee agreement?"

"Yes. Specify the scope of the project and include that we will educate the employee benefits administrator about particulars, to assist in implementation."

"Is there a special billing procedure?"

"No."

"When do you want to review the plan?"

"I would like to see it in draft a few days before I meet with the client."

"When will you meet with the client?"

"November 20."

"Are there any assumptions or specifications I should know about?"

"Generally, the company wants to encourage the executives to remain until retirement, but because of the stressful nature of the industry, normal retirement can be as early as 55."

"Who may I contact for the information I need?"

"Contact the chief financial officer. He is privy to our assignment and will be eligible to participate in the plan."

See Figure 6.3 for items that should be incorporated into the case flow chart in light of these questions and responses.

FIGURE 6.3: SAMPLE FLOW CHART ENTRIES

Execution of the Project

Incorporate into Case Flow Chart:

Update: 11/8

MATTER	ASSIGNMENT DATE	PRIORITY RANK	MAJOR TASK	MAJOR TASK	DUE DATE
Supp. Ret. Plan	11/8	7*	Call CFO	Draft	11/18-Supervising Attorney 11/20-Client

*after fee agreement drafted and CFO contacted, priority rank decreases to 7 for 3-4 days

CONSTRUCT WORK PLAN

Subdivide project into tasks and budget time:

1. Fill in assignment notes.
2. (a) Review files and research to determine questions for chief financial officer (CFO)
   (b) Prepare fee letter
3. (a) Obtain specifications from CFO
   (b) Submit fee letter to supervising attorney for review
4. (a) Draft plan, election, and beneficiary designation
   (b) Discuss with CFO
5. Submit for review
6. Revise and complete; prepare cover letter?
7. Follow up with executive vice president
8. Educate employee benefits administrator

If you anticipate that the client or supervisor must reach some decision upon your completion of a task and before proceeding to the next task or in order to select between alternatives, indicate such a decision point between tasks and mark it on the timeline.

To prepare a checklist to carry out a task, list major elements of the task to the extent possible. In thinking about the dimensions of each task, anticipate whether one or more of them must be addressed earlier than others because of required lead time. Listing the areas of research and information needed from the CFO should prompt the associate to realize that the CFO may require time to obtain some of the information, particularly that which involves a policy decision. Further, the CFO may be out of town or otherwise unavailable for one or more days. If the activities composing a task depend upon the outcome of earlier activities, then it is often useful to diagram the task and to periodically reassess the timeline.

For example, Task number 2(a) is to determine questions for the CFO, and items to research to prepare questions. These include:

Client's objectives

Eligibility (class or specific persons; what about subsidiaries?)

Who will be administrator or administrative committee?

Yield formula — and check whether less for separation from service

How does the company want to define form of benefit payment upon death, disability?

How does the company want to define "retirement"?

Frequency of statements of accounts

Vesting schedule for employer supplements

Effective date

Update research on applicability of ERISA

§ 6.03(c) Monitor Progress, Adjust Work Plan

Monitoring means comparing actual time and performance of major tasks with work plan estimates and the timetable.

Here are keys you can adapt to manage an assignment as departures from estimates occur, depending on assignment complexity and your role, level of accountability, and authority.

- Identify the departure from estimated time or changes in strategy or in major tasks from what was expected.
- Determine whether the departure will be significant — assess the implications to supervising attorney, client, and your own workload.
- If significant, perform a trade-off analysis. That is, identify and evaluate the feasibility of alternative adjustments or courses of action.

1. If actual time required will exceed that estimated, assess:
   - ⇨ Whether the result can be reached another way without incurring delay
   - ⇨ Whether delay is acceptable to supervising attorney and clicnt
   - ⇨ What new schedule you can meet
   - ⇨ What the additional time will cost the client (or the firm if fee is fixed)

- What resources would decrease or eliminate the additional time needed
- Whether the client would receive added value from the increased time and cost
- Whether the increase in time will accelerate your learning curve
- How you can integrate the schedule/timetable change into your workload

2. If strategy, major tasks, or work product will depart from what was expected or planned, assess:
   - How else the objective can be reached
   - What the advantages and disadvantages are for the client
   - How the change will affect estimated time and/or costs

After you have completed your analysis and arrived at a recommendation, confer with the supervising attorney. *See* § 6.05 [Part II, Expectation No. 6: "Communicate Progress and Status"].

§ 6.03(d) Missing Information and Resources

To sensibly create and carry out a work plan, obtain information critical to a meaningful analysis. An analysis and work product based upon hypothetical facts because important information is missing seldom benefits anyone. The work product may contain good preliminary research but, as a work product, is probably useless until further developed. New lawyers quickly spot what facts are missing, but often fail to look at a file soon enough to plan and estimate lead time needed to gather missing information and to avert preparation crises.

If they notice in time that information is missing, new lawyers often omit the next step: weighing the costs and benefits of obtaining the missing information. In evaluating the degree to which you need to find missing information, the cost of time and the effect of delay must be weighed against the expected benefits of the information — such as a more meaningful response, additional choices, or opportunities — in the context of the supervising attorney's expectations and the client's objective.

If the lawyer concludes that data is needed, the next step is to locate it. A new associate often fails to consider how to gather information which is not in the client file or in the library, other than by asking the supervising attorney. In many situations, however, the supervising attorney is neither the only nor the best source of factual information.

Locating missing information generally requires two steps. First, determine a primary source and one or more secondary sources. Rarely is there only one source of information. File correspondence and documents may refer to primary and secondary sources of the information you seek, or another attorney who has handled similar matters or knows the client may give you suggestions. Second, decide which sources to contact or use. If it is not appropriate to contact a person who is the primary source, decide which of the secondary sources to contact and confirm your proposed action with the supervising attorney. If you can foresee the need to contact resources, cover this with the supervising attorney when the assignment is given to avoid delays later on.

CONSIDER:

Suppose the firm is competing for a prospective client's business and will submit a proposal on how it would approach the project and accomplish the result. The first task is to secure background information about the company. Good beginning sources for public companies are the latest annual report to shareholders and proxy statement. These materials provide information on ownership, management, directors, compensation of the five most highly compensated executive officers, identity of the company's accounting firm, relevant financial highlights, new products, pending litigation, and registration statements. Computer data base searches for report data, relevant newspaper stories, and litigation can also highlight planning needs or legal difficulties the company is experiencing. Often these investigative tasks can be delegated to an experienced legal assistant, after deciding the scope of information wanted.

CONSIDER:

You are given a litigation assignment to draft interrogatories to determine how the plaintiff company stored a chemical product that your client, now the defendant, manufactured during the months in issue. In structuring the questions, you discover that they could go on and on if all possible storage procedure details are covered. Some of the inquiries are preliminary and consume too many of the 25-question maximum permitted by the jurisdiction's local rules governing discovery. You would like to eliminate some of the preliminary questions and rework others, but you need more knowledge of the industry. How do you go about obtaining the background you need? You might consider contacting a source in the client company, or one of its customers, and then clear what you propose to do with the supervising attorney. (Here, of course, we are talking about obtaining background information; factual issues should not be decided on the basis of these sources: you want the plaintiff's response.)

CONSIDER:

A supervising attorney assigns a research project on Wednesday that is due on the following Tuesday. The associate opens the file late Thursday afternoon and realizes that there is no information on the amount and nature of common stock ownership in excess of five percent. The supervising attorney left the city earlier that afternoon for an out-of-state meeting.

What are the options?

One option is to move on to another project, setting this assignment aside until Monday. What if, however, the associate learns on Monday that the supervising attorney will not return to the office until midday Tuesday? Some new lawyers adopt the "word from the mount" mentality: if the supervising attorney is unavailable, paralysis sets in until he or she returns. Another choice is to formulate an analysis in the hypothetical "what if" format. The hypothetical conclusion, however, may be to no avail, despite its merit as preliminary research: the client expects a *real* answer, a workable solution. Hence, the supervising attorney cannot formulate an overall strategy because it depends on this piece.

A better approach is to determine likely sources first. Then, if you have not had direct client contact, ask the supervisor's secretary to ask, when the supervisor calls in, whether you ought to contact the client or the secondary source. If the supervising attorney does not call in on Friday, or does not respond to the question, find out if others have worked with the client (and supervising attorney) and ask their advice.

CONSIDER:

An associate receives an assignment in May which requires locating and interviewing an expert witness. The trial is set for October. The associate knows that the type of expert needed will probably be a professor at a local university. When should the associate contact candidates and make a selection?

If the associate waits until June to begin making inquiries, faculty members may be on limited summer schedules and the associate will have trouble finding an appropriate expert in time. Procrastination yields predictable panic in the face of governing procedural rules, strategic assessments, and practical scheduling realities. Procedures may demand endorsement of the expert within a certain period of time before trial. An alert associate will review the file when the assignment is given and make a diary entry accordingly to avoid this (predictable) dilemma.

CONSIDER:

A second year associate is assigned to prepare a personal injury case for trial and is given the name of an out-of-state physician as a potential expert. The associate contacts the physician and sends appropriate data for the physician to conduct an analysis and prepare a report. The pretrial order must be filed in 90 days. When would you contact the physician again to follow up?

What actually happened?

Three days before the pretrial order was due, the associate called the physician's office to find out why the report had not been sent. The associate had not contacted the physician since sending the data and did not know the physician's opinion. (Yes, you read this correctly.) The physician was out of town and the physician's secretary informed the associate that the report had been mailed three days earlier. What should the associate do now? This associate asked the secretary to telecopy the report draft to the firm. The secretary replied that the office did not have a telecopier but agreed to send it by express mail. Since it was almost 5:00 p.m. in that time zone, she mailed it the following day.

On the day the pretrial order was due, the copy of the draft arrived. The associate noted, however, that it failed to address two critical issues. The Doctor was still unavailable. The associate decided to list the physician as an expert witness. (Opposing counsel had refused to agree to a motion for extension and the judge had denied the associate's motion.)

COMMENT

The lawyer could have easily prevented this outcome by following up periodically with the physician. Some new lawyers, not having juggled several matters before, neglect to follow up on one case until they are facing a crisis, because they are concentrating on another matter. Even failing that, the associate could have requested a contact in a law firm in the city where the doctor's office was located to obtain and telecopy the report.

APPLYING THIS EXPECTATION TO YOUR RESPONSIBILITIES

Manage your assignments effectively by creating a work plan, monitoring progress, adjusting the work plan, and delegating appropriate activities to your secretary:

Break projects into manageable parts.

Organize the file.

Construct a timetable and budget time.

Create checklists to carry out major tasks.

Enter tasks onto to do lists.

Assess benefit and cost of obtaining missing information.

Compare actual time and performance with what was expected.

Identify and assess impact of anticipated departures from estimates.

Evaluate course of action, alternatives. (See § 6.04.)

Make recommendation. (See §§ 6.04, 6.05.)

---

§ 6.04 EXPECTATION NO. 5: STAY ON TRACK BY THINKING BROADLY AND NARROWLY

It is up to you to periodically check that your approach is on track to reach the objective of the assignment; ask yourself why you are doing what you are doing.

You are now applying your analytical capabilities in the context of the client's objective. The following questions and discussion highlight three areas to include in gauging whether you are developing workable solutions and responsive work products.

Have I investigated relevant new issues?

Have I developed workable alternatives and recommendations?

Have I adapted forms to meet the client's objective?

§ 6.04(a) Be Alert to New Issues

The supervising attorney may not identify or discuss all issues that might need to be researched and analyzed. He or she may not have anticipated what you would find. If research and analysis leads you to another relevant line of inquiry, do not disregard it simply because the supervising attorney did not address it when making the assignment. Anticipate tasks that almost certainly will need to be tackled soon. If you are unable to judge whether to investigate the issue or how to proceed, or to identify a major issue outside of your area of substantive specialization, discuss it with the supervising attorney. *See* § 6.05 [Part II, Expectation No. 6: "Communicate Progress and Status"]. First, however, think through how you would proceed before seeking his or her assessment. That is, show initiative to identify choices on how to proceed, anticipate the pros and cons of each, and decide which you believe is best.

CONSIDER:

An associate is asked to draft interrogatories to determine how the plaintiff company stored a product that the client, the defendant, manufactured. While scanning some annotations, suppose the associate notices a situation in which a company had farmed out storage to an independent operator. The associate does not know whether the supervising attorney had considered and eliminated the possibility of third-party storage.

What went right?

This associate left a note for the supervising attorney that raised the possibility and requested a response only if the supervisor determined that questions about this alternative were inappropriate. The supervising attorney scribbled on the note that this inquiry should be made; he had not intended to infer that the storage location had been clarified.

Questions the lawyer asks or comments made by the client, coupled with familiarity with a client's business and industry, may prompt ideas for preventive measures or a related planning opportunity. *See* §§ 4.02, 4.03 [Part I, Expectations No. 13: "Understand the Client's Business" and No. 14: "Consider the Practical Aspects"].

CONSIDER:

An associate is assigned to pursue collection against a client's corporate customer and is given copies of the wholesaler-client's building material invoices and statements. Should the associate reviewing these documents also be thinking about steps the client could take to reduce problem accounts from now on?

The associate determined that the client should consider obtaining personal guarantees for certain categories of corporate orders to facilitate future collections. The associate also suggested that the current delinquency problems could be reduced if new invoice forms were drafted to show interest charges, and if the client tightened the credit application form and required a financial statement. The associate explained why the latter measure would also provide additional remedies if default occurred.

Result:

The client asked the associate to work with the credit manager to create new forms. Soon afterward, the client shared the associate's advice with a friend in a different business who had encountered similar problems and the firm was retained by that businessman.

When you have completed assigned work on a particular phase of a project and may not be involved in the remainder of it, record observations that will have continuing relevance to the supervising attorney and client. From your work, you may be in a unique position to anticipate some problems or identify additional planning opportunities that may arise. Your supervisor and whoever picks up the next phase will appreciate some background and your assessment of what could lie ahead.

CONSIDER:

The associate has finished drafting documents for the sale of a commercial building by a financial consulting firm to the firm's client, a real estate company. The supervising attorney mentioned a few days ago that the client and the consulting firm are negotiating joint venture. The client has purchased several commercial properties nationwide and wants to engage the consulting firm to structure the financial terms for the client's large commercial tenants. They expect to complete their negotiations and want an agreement drafted in a few days.

The associate has had numerous conversations with the client and the consulting company while drafting the transaction documents. During these conversations the associate observed that the two companies have very different decision-making philosophies: the consulting company moves slowly and involves each executive in the approval process for large financial packages. In contrast, the client's decisions are usually made by the president alone. Because the supervising attorney has not dealt with the financial consulting company before, the associate mentions this observation. The supervisor considers this practical operational factor in handling the new joint venture agreement.

§ 6.04(b) Develop Workable Alternatives, Recommendations

Clients and supervising attorneys usually expect more than an answer to the question, "Can we do it?" Your job does not end with "yes" or "no." If your answer is "yes," then the next question may be, "Do you think this is the best way to do it?" If your answer is "no," they usually want your assessment of "How else can we do it?" "What are the advantages and disadvantages of those alternatives?" Or, "What are the risks if we proceed?" Suppose you are asked whether a specific form will work in a transaction and you determine that it will not — as is. Next determine whether you can work with the form, make changes, and use it. If not, can you find another form to adapt? A client does not want to pay for the response, "No, that won't work. . . ." without exploration of alternatives that may work. *See* § 6.06 [Part II, Expectation No.7: "Make Your Work Product Useful"]. And, generally, the billing attorney probably would not have made the assignment if he or she did not believe there would be some way to reach the client's goal.

To address these questions, think about what the client ultimately wants to do. *See* § 2.02 [Part I, Expectation No.1: "Understand What The Client Wants To Do"]. What is the relative importance of those elements that are causing the problem? Can you restructure those elements and still reach the ultimate goal of accomplishing the transaction? "What if. . . .?" The essence of a "what if" analysis is the ability to go beyond your initial assessment of the most likely outcome, based on the planned course of action or current state of affairs. It is the ability to anticipate the alternative future events or conditions that may occur, to analyze the relative probabilities of occurrence, to determine their impact, actions the client can take, and then to develop and recommend the most effective strategies to reach the ultimate goal. Performing a series of "what if" analyses requires attention to practical factors as well as legal factors: business conditions and trends, the client's predisposition, priorities, psychological needs, concerns, economic information, and so forth. *See* § 4.03 [Part I, Expectation No. 14: "Consider The Practical Aspects"].

CONSIDER:

The lawyer, as an *ex officio* board member of a client company, is asked to give his evaluation of whether to issue stock to employees to increase productivity and promote loyalty. The lawyer assesses the hidden costs. They include minority shareholder rights on sale of the business, dilution of the founding group's interest, and disappointment over lack of opportunity for any dramatic rise in value if the company does not go public. The lawyer explores with the client whether issuance of actual or phantom stock really would foster increased productivity and loyalty. Then the lawyer expresses alternative incentives to increase productivity and promote loyalty.

CONSIDER:

A project owner is sued on a mechanic's lien by a supplier-subcontractor. The owner has the opportunity to bring a third-party action against the general contractor for failure to pay contract funds to this supplier. The attorney can include in the action all other claims the owner has against the general contractor for additional amounts that are not the subject of the plaintiff's mechanic's lien action. The lawyer discusses with the owner the legal consequences of failing to include these additional claims: they are compulsory claims and are waived if they are not included in the third party action. The client explains that he or she is still involved in negotiations with the general contractor for remaining work. The lawyer and client discuss negotiating strategy and the lawyer explains the deadlines for deciding on whether to include the claims in the third party action.

§ 6.04(c) Adapt Forms

Forms provide a starting point from which to spot issues and problems that may need to be considered, to identify alternative solutions, and to craft language. A substantial amount of time frequently can be saved by searching the firm's centralized internal work product/precedent file or data base. Ask firm members whether they have developed forms for the subject you are handling. Be advised, however, that the person you ask is probably not thoughtfully reflecting on the situation you pose and is merely suggesting that a particular form or file may be helpful.

Do not use forms indiscriminately: each form was developed to meet another client's objective and may have represented a compromise at that. Forms developed by firm members, however, *may* reflect their or the firm's standards for quality and preferences for handling problems. Commercially available forms can also be useful where firm members have not developed a document. However, unlike the firm's forms from which reference can be made to the file for the context in which the form was developed, the context of commercial forms is unknown and compliance with current law may be unclear.

APPLYING THIS EXPECTATION TO YOUR RESPONSIBILITIES

Maintain your focus on the client's objective:

Whenever possible, set the analysis aside and then consider whether you

Investigated relevant new issues.

Developed and evaluated alternative strategies.

Examined analysis and forms from client's, adversary's, or related party's perspectives and objectives.

Adapted forms to accomplish the objective and priorities.

Made workable recommendations.

---

§ 6.05 EXPECTATION NO. 6: COMMUNICATE PROGRESS AND STATUS

Good communication among the supervising attorney and others assigned to a matter is imperative for good client service. As the associate assigned to a matter, you must take initiative to keep the supervising attorney abreast of developments in the project or case. This is an integral part of your management of the assignment and the supervising attorney's management of the matter. It gives the supervising attorney an opportunity to timely assess whether strategy should be adjusted and to communicate progress to the client, who may otherwise feel that the firm considers his or her business unimportant. In addition, it behooves the new lawyer to check in to ensure that he or she is proceeding on course and is informed of developments impacting on the project.

Each supervising attorney has requirements, or possibly some idiosyncrasies, about being kept up on a matter's status. The expectation may be that you will supply a comment in the hall, a note, or a formal status memorandum. When receiving the assignment, the assigned attorney should clarify what is expected by the request, "Keep me up to date. . . ." Or, ask others who have worked with the supervising attorney about what he or she has expected in the past. Do not expect the supervising attorney to track your progress by looking through your time slips. Unless otherwise instructed, you should follow some generally accepted and well-considered practices. Copy the supervising attorney on correspondence you have prepared and sent. If you meet with the client or another person outside the firm on an assignment, prepare a file memo summarizing the meeting and copy the supervising attorney. When you conduct telephone conferences, summarize them in a file memo. If you take depositions, memo the file with your assessment. After internal strategy conferences, memo the file. (Using a tear-off pad of prepunched file memo forms makes this procedure easy to follow.) Additional "checkpoints" that generally note when you need to communicate project status, depending upon the context of a project, include:

- Number of hours
- A period of time
- Completion of a designated major task or nonoccurrence of an event
- Need for clarification, guidance, or judgment
- Significant increase in time over estimate
- Material change in cost or strategy
- Mistakes

§ 6.05(a) Number of Hours, Period of Time, Completion of a Designated Major Task, or Occurrence/Nonoccurrence of an Event

Litigation and other legal activities are not isolated economic events: they are related to the client's plans, ongoing operations, and changes in circumstances. Thus, the assigned attorney should check with the supervising attorney periodically to find out if there have been new developments that affect the assignment. A client's activities are not suspended upon assignment of a project; between the engagement process and completion of a work product, the client may take actions or face related problems that affect the assignment and may require a mid-course correction. Indeed, the client may be changing a specification on the way back to his office from the initial meeting.

Projects of substantial duration in which you have little or no direct client contact require that you be especially diligent to confirm your planned course of action periodically with the supervising attorney. Suppose, for example, the supervising attorney believes a complex litigation matter which you are preparing for trial will settle and directs you to place further pretrial preparation on hold. You must recheck the status frequently so you will be ready to gear up if negotiations falter. Or suppose the supervising attorney, on instructions from the client, directs an associate to make exhaustive efforts to prepare for trial. A month later the client sees an important opportunity to resume business dealings with the "other side." Perhaps the client company had wanted to teach the other side a lesson — and has succeeded sooner than anticipated. Flexibility becomes the key factor. Everything can change with a phone call. Do not assume that an assignment given is an assignment written in stone.

When receiving assignments, find out, if possible, the time intervals at which you will be expected to report progress or status to the supervising attorney. Also determine whether a handwritten note, a more formal written report, or an oral report is expected. (The supervising attorney's secretary or legal assistant is a valuable resource.) A supervising attorney may also expect to be informed of meetings an associate sets so he or she has the option to attend. For example, sufficient notice might consist of a note saying: "I'm planning to meet with the client's CPA on such and such a date to. . . . Let me know if you want to attend." The scheduled meeting date should also be entered in the docket control system, and on the associate's and supervising attorney's calendars.

§ 6.05(b) Need for Clarification, Guidance or Judgment

CONSIDER:

A general counsel engages a partner to prepare for and handle a hearing before the National Labor Relations Board. The partner delegates the case to an associate who proceeds to obtain a favorable result. The associate does not contact the client following the hearing.

Result:

The client is later annoyed that he did not receive a telephone call about the outcome, and because the associate incurred time to produce an eight page written report.

What went wrong?

Two days after the hearing the associate dictated the report to the client and submitted it to the partner. The partner was surprised to see the report because he assumed that the associate had related the outcome to the client immediately. In other engagements, the partner's communication with this client has been informal.

Comment:

The associate should have reported the result to the partner and clarified whether the partner intended to call the client or if he was expected to follow up with the client and prepare a report. The client's ultimate dissatisfaction in the wake of a successful result could have been easily avoided.

What if the hearing had been unsuccessful? It is generally prudent for an associate to ask the supervising attorney how to handle this situation.

When seeking the supervising attorney's judgment or guidance, *first analyze the problem yourself and prepare to recommend possible solutions.* For example, "The judge wants us to meet in conference in chambers or by telephone conference. I have not appeared in her court before. Here's the situation. . . . The other side wants to handle it by telephone conference. I think that we should insist on meeting in chambers so we can educate the judge about. . . . What do you think?"

CONSIDER:

To prepare an appellate brief, the firm's appellate lawyer first meets with the trial lawyers and then formulates a timetable. After researching points of error and composing arguments, the appellate attorney again confers with the trial lawyers to validate particulars of the brief. They determine that one point of error is stronger than another.

§ 6.05(c) Significant Increase over Time Estimate

Occasionally only through work on a matter does it become clear that the time allocated for completion of a task or project will not be sufficient. You are well advised to notify the supervising attorney before the deadline. A supervisor should not have to track down an assigned attorney on the due date to learn of a delay and the reason for it. In any event, notice allows the supervising attorney to assess the impact of the projected delay and options, and to determine whether to adjust the deadline, enlist help, reassign the case, or timely discuss the problem with the client.

If you believe the supervising attorney may be unaware of the reason that a project has taken significantly more time than expected, consider attaching a note to it explaining the reason for delay. This information may help the supervising or billing attorney to judge how to bill the client for the work. It may also help the supervising attorney evaluate your work.

§ 6.05(d) Material Change in Cost or Strategy

CONSIDER:

An unanticipated problem arises on the project assigned to an associate. In estimating the time that would be spent to continue on the course of action, the associate determines that, unless the problem is resolved fully in favor of the client, the cost would exceed the amount of recovery under the most likely outcome.

What would you do?

The associate informs the supervising attorney of his assessment based on the current status and furnishes a rough estimate of fees the client would incur under best, probable, and worst case scenarios. This information positions the supervising attorney to timely discuss the situation with the client's general counsel. *See also* § 4.07 [Part I, Expectation No. 17: "Use Economic Sense"].

§ 6.05(e) Mistakes

We all make them. *Do not hide them.* When you realize that you have made a mistake, immediately call it to the supervising attorney's attention. It may be cured if acted on promptly. As time passes, the client or others may have taken actions that make resolution of the mistake more difficult or impossible.

**APPLYING THIS EXPECTATION
TO YOUR RESPONSIBILITIES**

Communicate progress and status to the supervising attorney at key checkpoints. Determine which apply to each of your active matters:

Number of hours.

Period of time.

Completion of designated major task or occurrence/nonoccurrence of an event.

Need for clarification, guidance, or judgment.
—First think through the problem and recommend a solution.

Significant change from time estimate, cost or strategy.
—Anticipate, report departures from estimates or expectations.

Mistake
—Immediately call to the supervising attorney's attention.

---

§ 6.06 EXPECTATION NO. 7: MAKE YOUR WORK PRODUCT USEFUL

The supervising attorney expects a completed, useful work product that is responsive to the specific goals of the client. Your work product, oral or written, should represent you as your best effort. If what you submit is not your best effort, you only hurt yourself at review time.

Some work products are prepared only for the supervising attorney; others are intended for the client as well. Therefore, consider your audience and how the supervising attorney plans to use your work product to inform, solve problems for, persuade, or otherwise provide service to the client. Organize and prepare appropriately. A supervising attorney may decide to give the client a copy of a memorandum that answers a question, analyzes "what if's" to arrive at workable options, or reports telephone conversations or interviews — particularly if it is in a format that does not have to be reworked first.

The supervising attorney expects to receive a work product memorandum that answers a question, assesses how to use a case, creatively evaluates alternatives, recommends a solution, and so forth; he or she wants help — and expects you to provide something a client will pay for! *See* § 6.04 [Part II, Expectation No. 5: "Stay On Track By Thinking Broadly and Narrowly"]. Some new lawyers retain an academic approach and regard an assignment, consciously or unconsciously, as an exercise intended to demonstrate to the supervising attorney a grasp of technical research apart from its application to the real problem. They view the client as an abstraction and fail to consider that the supervising attorney *requires* an answer for the client. (When drafting your "questions presented," check whether they are phrased in the abstract. If they do not incorporate facts, consider whether your analysis and writing are focused on the client's goal or problem.)

In preparing a memorandum of analysis, remember that the supervising attorney will not be as familiar with your research and analysis as you are. He or she may be able to devote only a limited amount of time and attention to digesting its essence and to reviewing the facts and cases on which it is based. Although the supervising attorney may want to review your analytical process at some time, the immediate question upon your completion of the product is usually a variation of, *"What did you find?" "What do you think we should do and why?" "What if we do this . . . what if we do that?" "How significant is that problem for us?"* Or *"What is the controlling case law? Can we use it?"* Anticipate and answer these types of questions. Place yourself in the supervising attorney's shoes as you work on the project and ask yourself: If I had delegated this assignment, is this work product what I want and need to move on to the next step? Does it answer the question? Can I use it now and call the client? Can I give this to the client? (Or, would the client wonder, "What did he say?") Also make a note of areas that you have not investigated or analyzed but which may bear consideration at a later stage.

When possible, set aside your work product for a day; after an interval, it becomes easier to reread the material from your reader's perspective and then to make it clearer. Many firms or individual departments have incorporated examples of what they consider outstanding memoranda organization into a manual or form file. The following are several guidelines: state the objective or question presented, then a brief answer or summary recommendation, and between two and five key reasons to support your summary or answer. Begin the body of the work product with a statement of facts, and assumptions, followed by the analysis, and conclusion. The conclusion of your research is often based upon many factors, but the written and oral communication of your conclusion should be clear and concise.

New lawyers who view the work product they submit for review as "just a draft" tend to postpone the essential steps of: checking transition, cite-checking, proofreading, putting court documents into filable form, and refining organization, sentence structure, and grammar. As a result, they present the supervising attorney with a half-baked recommendation or leave problems unresolved that, given more thought, could have been successfully tackled. As discussed earlier, in § 6.01 [Part II, Expectation No. 2: "Understand and Clarify Assignments"], a supervising attorney's request to see a draft does not translate into anything less than a request for a completed product that is ready to go on letterhead. The reasons a supervising attorney asks for a draft may vary, but they usually relate to further thought or work that he or she plans to put into the matter, not to the associate's second chance to polish the work product.

Sometimes a supervising attorney will make changes to your work product without explanation or even any mention. Check the file or computer files containing prior versions to find out if changes have been made and to review them. If you do not understand the purpose of a change, make a note and ask during a later opportunity. Also consider asking the supervisor's secretary to save the redlined copy for you, to make your review easier.

§ 6.06(a) Work Product for Client

1. Place yourself behind the reader's desk. Do not assume that the reader knows the subject matter as well as you do. Consider drafting your summary answer deductively, unless instructed otherwise. To test it, ask yourself whether, standing alone, it is sufficient for the reader to reach a decision, take action, and understand what has been accomplished. At all times, the client should be able to relate your rationale and support back to the objective and to the recommendation or conclusion.

Express your conclusion, if possible, from a positive perspective — it moves the reader closer to reaching the objective — such as how to do something. What if your conclusion is that the client's proposal will not work? Can it be done another way? To avoid being perceived as unhelpful or a deal-buster, you might include in your analysis statements illustrating other means to reach a goal if specified elements in the proposal were changed or certain steps were taken.

2. Assume that the reader may be able to devote only a limited amount of time and attention to your presentation. Consider: If a memorandum exceeds 6-10 pages, would a table of contents be helpful to your reader?

3. Order the key points in the body of the document consistently with their sequence in the answer; do not bury them.

4. Present the legal analysis in the context of what is significant to the client, such as helping the client to arrive at a business decision. Clients want to know what the lawyer's advice does for them; clients are not interested in the tortuous process that the lawyer follows in converting that client's goals into legal concepts to which the attorney can apply legal principles in arriving at suggestions for resolution of problems or recommendations to further those goals. Clients are not interested in theoretical points. They *are* interested in those suggestions and recommendations.

When writing to inside counsel, the ultimate question is still whether the advice will work from a business perspective. In addition, however, you must show your analytical skill, in a manner similar to the method used in writing for a supervising attorney. *See* § 4.09 [Part I, Expectation No. 20: "Understand the Expectations of A Corporate Law Department"].

5. Avoid a tendency to share all details.

6. Clearly set forth and establish priority among the material facts and assumptions upon which you base your analysis and recommendations.

7. Note where any material information is missing, indicate when you expect to receive it, and describe its anticipated effect on your conclusion.

8. Label legal considerations, practical and business factors, and caveats so that the client is clear about these distinctions.

9. Use the client's language. *See* § 3.06 [Part I, Expectation No. 11: "Use the Client's Language"]. Use this opportunity to show familiarity with the client's business, and with the way the client operates and thinks. If the client processes concepts through analogies, use them. If your primary support for the conclusion is complex, consider using graphics or illustrations and short paragraphs.

10. Clearly mark each draft by number and date to avoid confusion.

Consider this deductively structured summary directed to the client:

Objective: How to comply with health care continuous coverage law — effective for the 1987 plan year

Summary: Adjust plan to offer an employee the right to buy continued health coverage (group rates) at termination (except if terminated for gross misconduct) for himself, a dependent, a child who is no longer a dependent, and a divorced spouse.

Points:

- Law requires the plan to add this option. B Corporation's current group health benefits already include coverage for widowed spouses which is required by the new law, but do not offer continuous coverage in these other situations.
- In the plan, B Corporation fully pays the employee's coverage; an employee can elect to cover spouse and dependents at cost of that additional coverage according to the carrier's rates.
- B Corporation may charge up to 102% of cost to the plan for any continued coverage elected.
- Numbers on cost to the plan for continued coverage are being prepared by the carrier in consultation with us and the employee benefits administrator, and are expected at the end of the month.

- B Corporation can use the requirement that notice be given when the new benefit is offered as an opportunity to communicate to its employees the value of current benefits and this enhancement.

§ 6.06(b) Requests for Proposal

More and more, prospective corporate clients are selecting a law firm to handle a complex transaction or litigation based on the firm's response to a Request for Proposal [RFP] (or Request for Quotation). If you are assigned to draft the response to an RFP, structure your presentation in the order directed by the request. If, however, the request is less formal, is characterized as an interview process, or does not specify an order, the following design suggestions may be helpful.

Cover the firm's understanding of the project; the firm's approach; the lead lawyer's relevant experience; the qualifications of attorneys and legal assistants who will work on the project under the direction of the lead lawyer, if applicable; the firm's background; and the lead lawyer's response to questions on fees, costs, and billing method. Give the client a sense of the firm's unique capability to handle the project. Demonstrate some knowledge of the client's industry; convey an impression that the firm is interested, has given thought to the client's objective, and has a sense of the problem and a proposed timetable. Highlight the lead lawyer's case management philosophy. If the prospective client seeks full service representation, explain how anticipated projects will be cost-effectively managed and coordinated.

To effectively prepare the response, you should conduct some preliminary research about the company. Ask the client contact for clarification of the purpose of the project. An RFP often does not spell out critical background information that is needed to understand priorities, concerns, or expectations. Research should also be conducted, as directed by the lead lawyer, to anticipate and prepare for questions he or she will be asked during an interview.

APPLYING THIS EXPECTATION TO YOUR RESPONSIBILITIES

Determine expected work product

Know its purpose and recipients

To make it useful, ask yourself:

Does it answer the question?

Can the supervising attorney use it?

For correspondence or a memorandum intended for the client or which may be shown to the client —

Is it written for the client?

If the answer is "no, that won't work" —

Do you address alternatives?

If the answer is "yes, that will work" —

Do you determine whether that is the best solution?

---

§ 6.07 EXPECTATION NO. 8: DEVELOP MEETING AND TELEPHONE SKILLS

Client-oriented lawyers translate their legal work into client service. Supervising attorneys expect new lawyers to possess or to develop skills to handle client contact positively and productively in situations they will likely encounter. A first year lawyer may be asked to contact the client by telephone, to convey status by letter, to communicate developments or request information, to attend conferences with the supervising attorneys, and to work with a client's in-house lawyers or staff.

§ 6.07(a) Participating in Client Meetings with the Supervising Attorney

As associates, your first direct exposure to a client may be at a meeting with the supervising attorney. As you make substantive preparations for a meeting, clarify with the supervising attorney what your role will be. Are you to handle part of a topic or will the supervising attorney indicate when you are to address or respond to a point? Are you there because you are expected to work on the next step? Will you need to elicit and discuss specific information at the meeting?

Your role must be clear to the client as well. A client does not understand the need for, or the function of, a second lawyer until he or she makes a contribution that the client perceives as meaningful. Thus, unless your role has been explained in advance by the supervising attorney, the client may assume that an unfamiliar lawyer is in attendance only as a trainee at the client's expense.

Whether your participation is limited or extensive, concentrate on establishing rapport with the client. Introduce yourself; observe the client's expression of interests; be alert for an opportunity to offer a comment or question on the client's art, community project, and or other interest. Seek to engage in a brief conversation before the meeting begins as an opportunity to create a good first impression and establish a measure of rapport. If the meeting takes place in a dinner setting, it is particularly important to carry the conversation periodically to give the supervising attorney a moment to think and to eat.

To prepare, some threshold information should be obtained before a meeting. Find out the:

Purpose for the meeting;

Intended result, actions;

Agenda;

Attendees;

Your role; and

Anticipated length of the meeting.

See Appendix H, Worksheet for Meeting Preparation.

§ 6.07(b) Your Meetings

Law schools do not give instruction on how to plan and conduct an effective meeting. More often than not, you are left to observe other lawyers, some of whom are not particularly skilled at planning and conducting meetings.

§ 6.07(b)(1) Have a Clear Purpose

Define the reason for a meeting. What should be accomplished? Many meetings are unnecessary. Again, unless you can identify a clear purpose for a meeting and what you expect to accomplish, the session is probably unnecessary or premature. The objective may best be handled in writing, over the telephone, or possibly by your unilateral action. For example, it may be easier to secure commitments on a one-to-one basis through separate telephone calls before holding a meeting. Politicians know the value of this kind of "lobbying" and decision making before the decision is formally made.

§ 6.07(b)(2) Prepare an Agenda

To accomplish your purpose and maintain control over the direction and progress of your meeting, prepare a written agenda of the topics you intend to cover. Have a specific objective for each item. You may be able to handle some preliminary items by telephone. Determine the order in which the topics should be addressed and set time limits for the meeting and for each topic.

Beginning the meeting with a noncontroversial item can often test the waters effectively, allowing you to adjust your strategy for the tougher topics. Place the more difficult topics after the "testing topics" to allow sufficient time to deal with and resolve them. Do not put off make-or-break items until the end, however. List them early on the agenda. If they cause an impasse, time spent on earlier items may have been wasted.

Consider whether you can accomplish more if you distribute discussion materials, as well as the agenda, in advance and how far ahead it should be done. Because written materials can contribute to the tone of the meeting, always evaluate their effect and how to package them.

§ 6.07(b)(3) Decide on Necessary Participants

Have a specific reason for including each person in the meeting. Determine who needs to agree or take action to accomplish your purpose. For example, if you are convening a negotiating session, determine whether each person has authority to negotiate at all. Sometimes the supervising attorney may wish to attend your meeting. Inform his or her secretary of the date, time, and purpose of each significant meeting and include it as an entry on the docket system.

§ 6.07(b)(4) Conduct the Meeting

It is important to construct an opening statement and preliminary observations or questions to set a tone conducive to achieving your purpose.

If you convene a meeting, you are the leader and are responsible for maintaining control over its direction and progress. Anticipate problems you may face in maintaining momentum or control, such as extraneous discussion or personal attacks that must be diffused early.

Problems of control can arise within your own camp as well as with other participants. Lawyers often painstakingly prepare clients about what to expect during the course of a meeting. In preparing experts in a litigation matter or outside advisors, however, the same lawyers frequently limit preparation to substantive issues and fail to talk with them about anticipated procedural difficulties, or the scope of their participatory roles. Expert witnesses or outside advisors focus on the facets of the matter requiring their respective assistance. Although the expert's comments are normally limited to a particular issue, an expert can sometimes offer an unsolicited analysis of the remainder of a transaction as viewed from his or her particular bias. To ensure that an expert understands his or her role in the meeting, spend some time discussing the meeting's purpose with the expert.

Thorough preparation in advance of any meeting will allow you to focus on the behavior of each participant and let you determine more effectively how to reach agreement or the action you desire. To orchestrate agreement, for example, demonstrate how each participant will benefit so that, at the conclusion of the meeting, each person willingly assumes responsibility for a task. If you are rehearsing your presentation as others speak, or you must concentrate unduly on your delivery, you will miss reactions to your ideas, strategies, or recommendations. Summarize points and decisions frequently to ensure that everyone understands the views presented.

§ 6.07(b)(5) Client Employees

Lawyers often neglect the employees the client has invited. Although these individuals may not be decision makers, they do influence the client and the client wants their opinions; otherwise they would not have been invited. Show an interest in their questions and comments and take care not to alienate them inadvertently. Learn each one's role and perspective, and consider how your recommendation or solution to a problem affects them. To the extent that your solution or recommendation will benefit them, communicate those benefits to them as a means of gaining their cooperation and support.

§ 6.07(b)(6) Closing the Meeting

When you have achieved your purpose, stop. Conclude the meeting on time with a summary of the planned action steps to be taken and a timetable. Ensure that each participant understands how assignments will affect the matter's progress. Coordinate responsibilities where possible to promote interim progress. Within twenty-four hours, prepare a memorandum of the meeting for yourself, including each attendee's concerns, biases, suggestions, and other information, even though some items no longer appear significant. This data may help you later if circumstances change. Also, send each participant a written summary of the assigned responsibilities, action steps, and timetable. (Make entries on your calendar, docket system, and To Do list, as appropriate.)

§ 6.07(c) Initiating a Call

Before placing the call, decide exactly what you want to accomplish, list the points you will cover and questions to ask, and gather the material you anticipate will be needed during the conversation. Do not wing it. The client is busy and will not welcome a second call to address points or questions that should have been covered the first time.

Respect your listener's time. When initiating a call, you might ask, "Do you have about five minutes to answer some questions I have about work papers you prepared for our client . . . ?" If the listener appears harried or preoccupied and unable to give you full attention, offer to call back and set up a telephone appointment.

Enter a telephone appointment on your calendar or day planner just as you would a scheduled meeting. Scheduling the return call will eliminate the round of telephone tag you may encounter if you respond, "Give me a call first thing in the morning." What does that mean? Effective use of a voice mail system also reduces telephone tag.

Small talk, while necessary to set the tone for a meeting, does not always serve that purpose in a telephone call. Generally, do not linger over pleasantries – get to the point. However, beginning a call on a positive note is important. It is annoying when a caller jumps in with questions that presume the listener has material relating to that matter on the desk and has been studying it immediately before the call. Worse, if your assignment is to gather information from a client, you are not likely to do well if you open with, "I don't think your deal is going to work, but I need some more information." What is the point? You have already decided it will not work.

If you are expecting someone to return a call, consider writing a note to yourself listing the points you intend to cover. When the call is returned, you will not find yourself scrambling to reconstruct what you called about or remembering only one of the several questions you intended to ask.

If you want to keep the phone call short, set the tone with, "Hello, thanks for returning my call. I called because. . . ." Compare this opening with, "Hi, how are you doing? Wasn't the game last night great?"

§ 6.07(d) Handling Incoming Client Calls

When a client calls to ask a question or discuss a matter, inexperienced associates often exhibit a range of reactions, frequently beginning with surprise. Some display confidence and judgment. Others are flattered and show a desire to demonstrate their knowledge; still others demonstrate their overwhelming concern over having to handle the call even before they know what it involves. The latter two frames of mind impair the ability to carefully listen to the client. Listen to a question and determine (1) whether the client expects an immediate answer and, if so, (2) whether it is appropriate to respond immediately or whether the question requires additional thought or research. Listening means blocking out your premature thoughts and concentrating on what is said.

If the client expects an answer immediately and you decide you are comfortable providing it, qualify your answer as needed to give yourself an opening for potential revision upon further reflection. For example, you can qualify the answer by saying, "If I think of anything that would change what we've discussed, I will call later today." A qualification goes a long way in preventing this painful experience: checking the support for the answer, finding it requires revision, calling the client, and receiving a surprised and irritated response that, "You said it was OK, so we did it."

There are ways to postpone an answer so that the client believes you understand the question, know how to go about finding an answer in a reasonable amount of time, and will get right on it. First, categorize the reason you should not or cannot respond immediately: "the question is complex and requires additional thought or research because. . . ." "I must check the file to find out. . . ." "I need to make a telephone call to. . . . to find out. . . ." Or, some other, similar comment. Second, estimate when you will call back with a response and tell the client when to expect a call.

The great majority of clients will respect your professional integrity if you frankly say you do not know the answer. Of course, you should couple your admission with whatever useful information you can give, such as the principles generally applicable in the area of the client's question — expressed in terms that are meaningful to the client. You will not impress these clients if you try to soft shoe around your present inability to answer the question. Consider also whether the client asked to speak with you as the supervising attorney's ear because he or she is unavailable. Sometimes a client's intent is only to ensure that the question is understood and will be relayed promptly.

CONSIDER:

The associate, who has occasionally assisted a partner on a client company's matters in conjunction with its legal department, receives a call from an operations manager. This manager runs the client's manufacturing line and has not dealt with the firm before. He requests a copy of an employment agreement the firm had drafted for the client company earlier in the year. The associate mentions her involvement in the drafting. The manager asks how the terms were developed and represents that he is entering into a similar arrangement with the company. The associate answers the question, agrees to furnish a copy, and sends it later that day.

What went wrong?

The issue was sensitive because the General Counsel and the President were restructuring that manager's responsibilities and compensation. The General Counsel learns of the firm's action and remarks to the President and says, "Who do they think manages the legal affairs of this company?"

Comments:

Inexperienced associates, as part of an outside counsel's team, must be sensitive to each client's policies, culture, operating style, and reporting relationships. If there is a developed legal department, *it* has the responsibility to provide legal advice to the corporation with whatever assistance it deems appropriate. *See* § 4.09 [Part I, Expectation No. 20: "Understand the Expectations of a Corporate Law Department"].

Although the associate's earlier contact had been with the legal department, the associate did not stop to think about protocol or to consider whether the manager had been authorized to call the firm.

Based on these factors and the nature of the request, the associate should have deferred a response and advised the partner of the conversation. Some clients have been known to call an associate for things they know a more experienced attorney would not give them.

§ 6.07(e) Making a "Cold Call"

If you have had little or no contact with the client before, this telephone conversation will form the client's first impression of you and will also influence his or her perception of the firm as a business. Therefore, before making the call, find out whether the supervising attorney has introduced your role by reference or expects you to handle your own introduction. If the client has been informed about your involvement and role, you need only give your name followed by something like, "I assist Terry in structuring and closing large commercial real estate transactions such as yours." This introduction should refresh the client's memory of the supervising attorney's reference to you.

If, however, the client is unaware of your involvement, a more extended introduction is usually in order (1) to assure the client that his or her attorney remains actively involved and interested; (2) to preliminarily demonstrate your qualifications to work on the project; and (3) to assure the client that you have already been briefed on the objective and the issues, and that you were asked to call.

APPLYING THIS EXPECTATION TO YOUR RESPONSIBILITIES

To prepare for a meeting, know:

Purpose of the meeting.

Intended result, actions.

Agenda.

Attendees.

Your role.

Anticipated length.

To handle a client's telephone questions:

Listen carefully to questions; block out premature thoughts. Then assess:

Whether the client is asking for your answer or the supervising attorney's.

If the client expects your answer,

when can you respond —

- Are you able to answer now —
  How sure are you of the answer?
- Qualify your answer appropriately so you can revise if necessary.
- Do you need time to respond — how much time do you estimate to prepare answer? What do you need to

do to develop an answer? Who else should be consulted in developing a response?

- Communicate to the client when to expect a response.
- Explain a step you need to take to respond (research, telephone calls, check file, etc.).

7

Long-Term Development: Planting the Seeds of Future Success

§ 7.01 EXPECTATION NO. 9: PLAN YOUR CAREER

Just as successful law firms set goals and devise strategies to achieve them, new lawyers must ask themselves, "What do I want to accomplish in 1 year, 2 years, 5 years, *et cetera*?" and take the initiative to chart their own professional development. And, consciously or not, most firms expect their associates to take the initiative in building skills for a successful career. Similar to the planning phases of other processes you have undertaken, career planning involves setting realistic, achievable long and short term goals, and developing strategies and tasks to reach them.

To begin setting your goals, absorb what is going on around you. Identify capabilities needed to become an able lawyer and to succeed in your law firm. You will find that successful lawyers possess multifaceted capabilities that often include managing a team of lawyers and legal assistants on significant client matters and developing clients, as well as contributing an important expertise, producing a designated amount of work, and honing legal writing, negotiating, and oral presentation skills. Also develop an awareness of economic realities influencing the firm's goals and strategies such as competition for clients and recruits, types of operating costs, its search for ways to increase efficiency, and investment made in new associate lawyers.

Determine how you can draw upon firm resources in carrying out career planning strategies. Assess how you can better use your supervising attorneys' guidance to develop substantive expertise and certain practical skills. For example, if you are in the litigation practice area, create an opportunity to observe your supervising attorney's courtroom skills. Prepare a list of factors to observe about his or her strategy and style. Then record your observations. Consider this sample format:

FIGURE 7.1: OPENING STATEMENT

FACTORS		OBSERVATIONS/ EXAMPLES
1. How does the lawyer present/introduce— the client?	⇨	
2. How does the lawyer refer to/handle		
• expected testimony	⇨	
• problems	⇨	
• pleadings, stipulated facts, etc.	⇨	

Also consider requesting that the supervising attorney attend and critique one of our negotiating sessions, a deposition, *et cetera.* Also locate and tap outside resources such as seminars and articles on effective speaking or negotiation that will be valuable tools in building capabilities, such as those listed below.

The following is a partial list of capabilities to evaluate as goals, or as strategic prerequisites to reach other goals you define:

Client Communications Skills

Client Development Skills

Courtroom/Arbitration Skills

Creativity

Delegation and Supervision Skills

Knowledge of an Industry's Practices, Problems, Trends

Legal Writing Skills: Advisory, Persuasive, Technical

Meeting Skills

Negotiation Skills

Oral Presentation Skills

Productivity/Workload and Time Management

Project Management Skills

Specialized Expertise — Mastering a Niche

For example, suppost an associate sets a goal of improving his oral presentation skills. Initial To Do's may consist of:

1. Observe presentation by [partner] on February 15.

2. Read these books: Mortimer J. Adler, *How To Speak, How To Listen)* (MacMillan 1983); Thomas Leach, *How To Prepare, Stage, and Deliver Winning Presentations* (AMACOM 1985).

3. Take a presentation skills course offered by . . . (1½ day session). (By March 15.)

Use this Worksheet as a tool to focus on and structure your career and professional development process. As you proceed, track your efforts, modify the tasks you have planned, and add other tasks.

Long Term Goals

____

____

Short Term Goals

____

____

Subdivide Goals Into Achievable Objectives.

Goal: ____

Objective: A. _________________________________

B. ____

C. ____

Strategy to Reach Objective A. ________________

____

List specific, realistic actions or tasks to carry out your strategy and determine how you will measure the results.

Assign dates by which action will be taken on each step; without assigning dates to intentions, it is likely that the actions will not be taken.

TASK	*TIMELINE
1. ____________________	____________________
2. ____________________	____________________
3. ____________________	____________________
4. ____________________	____________________
5. ____________________	____________________

*Record and track the nonbillable time spent in developing these skills.

Results of Tasks:

(Effective, Ineffective)

1. ______________________________
2. ______________________________
3. ______________________________
4. ______________________________
5. ______________________________

Strategy To Reach Objective B. ______________________________

____

TASK	TIMETABLE
1. ______________	______________
2. ______________	______________
3. ______________	______________
4. ______________	______________
5. ______________	______________

Results of Tasks:

(Effective, Ineffective)

1. ______________________________
2. ______________________________
3. ______________________________
4. ______________________________
5. ______________________________

Strategy to Reach Objective C. ______________________________

____

TASK	TIMETABLE
1. ____________	____________
2. ____________	____________
3. ____________	____________
4. ____________	____________
5. ____________	____________

Results of Tasks:

(Effective, Ineffective)

1. ____________________________
2. ____________________________
3. ____________________________
4. ____________________________
5. ____________________________

APPLYING THIS EXPECTATION TO YOUR RESPONSIBILITIES

To begin to chart your career, set short and long term goals.

Subdivide goals into achievable objectives.

Develop strategy to reach the objectives.

Plan and take specific, realistic — and measureable — actions.

Track the effectiveness of each step;

Make adjustments.

---

§ 7.02 EXPECTATION NO. 10: LAY THE FOUNDATION FOR BUSINESS DEVELOPMENT

As firms respond to external economic pressures, many are redefining their expectations of associate lawyers. More are placing client development responsibilities upon senior associates. Others are assessing an associate's capabilities to develop, manage, and retain clients when considering his or her potential for partnership levels. What are your firm's expectations?

New associates can begin to devote thought and preparation to this additional expectation by becoming aware of:

- How the firm generates business
- Firm's policies and procedures on screening and accepting new clients
- Future client development responsibilities
- Groundwork needed to lay in building client development capabilities

In some firms, associate lawyers are introduced to marketing activities and encouraged to participate. Other firms provide little notice of forthcoming client development responsibilities or preparatory direction. Therefore, the purpose of this chapter is to provide some ideas you can adapt, to undertake a focused, realistic planning process.

§ 7.02(a) Planning Prerequisite: Know Your Firm's Services and Client Markets

During the interview process, you evaluated various firms and their practices to determine which was the best choice. What qualities did the firm you selected project that gained your interest and set it apart from competitors?

More firms are identifying and targeting specific client markets and they are adapting their services to respond to the market needs. Some of the services cut across practice areas. For example, services offered to start up high technology companies require a range of expertise including corporate, intellectual property, tax, and financing. Other services, such as appellate representation, are performed within a single department.

Acquaint yourself with your firm's key services and "products" and with the benefits and features of each in terms that are meaningful to potential clients and referral sources. Read the firm's client newsletters. Attend firm and department breakfasts or luncheons. Notice what client meetings are scheduled for conference rooms. Also become aware of opportunities, problems, and trends in key clients' industries that shape or influence a client's objectives and expectations of the lead lawyer and the firm team. (*See* § 4.02 [Part I, Expectation No. 13: "Understand the Client's Business"] and § 7.02(i) ["Improve Practical Knowledge of an Industry"], below.) Your client-oriented research will help you refine and apply your substantive expertise and your delivery of services to respond to client needs. It will also assist you in identifying prospective clients and future referral sources among your contacts.

By finding out what other departments and practice areas do, you will also become better able to recognize when a client has a need for a service in which another department specializes. For example, a litigation client who is a real estate developer mentions to an associate working on the case that he will need financing for a transaction. The associate comments that the firm specializes in working closely with financial institutions on behalf of its clients to assure that all aspects of a transaction are appropriately structured and coordinated and cites an example from the firm's newsletter. He also informs the client that a team of real estate and financial services lawyers specializes in assisting in the formation of joint ventures between developers and institutional investors. The associate relates the conversation to the supervising attorney.

§ 7.02(b) Find Out How To Handle Prospective Client Inquiries

You will have opportunities to attract potential clients to the firm. A friend or relative may ask you to handle a matter, or may inquire whether your firm provides certain legal services. To respond in a businesslike manner, find out *now* what your firm's and department's policies, procedures, or expectations are in qualifying a potential client and submitting a matter to the office. Many firms have a new business committee to screen prospective matters; others require a partner's written approval for new clients. Also learn the categories of information that must be gathered from a prospective client to perform a search for potential conflicts of interest with current or former clients.

§ 7.02(c) Make a Good First Impression

Observe your rainmakers' styles. How do they attract clients? They begin with an attitude that every new acquaintance is a potential client or referral source. When they meet someone at an event, good business developers are alert to note his or her expression of a particular interest, hobby, and so forth, and to comment about it. They listen carefully, gather information, and show an interest in what the person shares with them. They also are quick to spot opportunities to tell people what they do and to cause them to share their business concerns and needs.

Before setting a meeting with a prospective client, they conduct research about his or her business and personal interests. They communicate effectively because they have gathered information about the client's needs before describing the benefits of their own services, and appear comfortable with the client's jargon and style. Your rainmakers make potential clients believe that they understand their goals and will devise a way to reach them lawfully. They convey such intangibles as trustworthiness, availability, concern, judgment, and their reputations. They have laid groundwork over a number of years; rarely have any rainmaker's beginning client development efforts been rewarded with the engagement of a major client.

To stimulate a potential client's and referral source's interest in your firm, always be prepared to answer the questions, "What business are you in?" "What kind of law do you practice?" Communicate the benefits of what you do and your firm's services to maximize the possibility that you will be remembered when a need arises. For example, if you mention that you are part of the business organization group that specializes in assisting business owners reach financing and estate planning objectives, you are more apt to prompt further inquiry than if you merely say, "I am a lawyer" or "I practice corporate law." Look over your firms brochure for examples of networthy transactions, as well as good descriptions of the firms practice areas, so you can respond effectively.

Instead of making "direct" inquiries (such as "What law firm do you use?" or "What legal problems are you facing?"), mention a recurring legal issue that others in the industry are facing. For example, to stimulate discussion of a potential client's needs the lawyer mentions to a new employer of a 200-employee business that a trap which many new employers encounter is failing to comply with overtime pay requirements for non-exempt personnel. Although that employer has taken care of this particular problem, the lawyer's comment may prompt him to mention a problem that he does have.

Exercise:

Situation 1: One of your civic organization colleagues, a district manager of a computer products company, introduces you to one of the company's staff lawyers at a reception.

How would you describe what you and your firm do?

____

____

Situation 2: You are seated next to a CPA at a luncheon hosted by the chamber of commerce.

How would you describe what you and your firm do?

____

____

Situation 3: Your child introduces you to a friend's parents at the school's parent-child breakfast.

How would you describe what you and your firm do?

____

____

Situation 4: A firm member introduces you to a potential client during an office tour. How would you describe what you and your firm do?

Situation 5: Last month you encountered this situation:

____

____

How would you describe what you and your firm do the next time? ____________________________________

____

§ 5.02(d) Develop Relationships with Counterparts in Client Organizations

A marketing activity that is closely aligned to an associate's practice is developing and maintaining relationships with counterparts in a client organization. A staff attorney or employee in a client company with whom you work can influence the client's perception of you and your firm. In addition, he or she may later become a decisionmaker or influencer in engaging outside counsel in that organization, or in another. A staff attorney in a client law department may be placed in charge of litigation, compliance, real estate transactions, and so forth, and be authorized to hire outside counsel as needed. For example, a lending officer with whom you work may switch companies and possess discretion to select counsel to handle environmental aspects of transactions involving real estate.

§ 7.02(e) Develop and Maintain Referral Sources

Other lawyers may become a significant source of

referrals as your career progresses. If your firm specializes in some services that a colleague's firm does not offer its clients, that lawyer may be ideally positioned to refer matters to you. Practitioners in other communities and regions may also be promising sources of referrals.

Develop relationships with peers in other businesses as well as with other lawyers. For example, advisors whose clients frequently need business or estate planning legal services include: CPAs, lenders, brokers, insurance agents, and financial consultants. Develop and maintain periodic contact with referral sources over a breakfast or lunch and by sending them articles that would interest them. In-house corporate counsel are also excellent sources of referrals as well as potential or existing clients. *See* § 4.09 [Part I, No. 20: "Understand the Expectations of a Corporate Law Department"].

List advisors with whom you are acquainted.

Name	Occupation
____________________	____________________
____________________	____________________
____________________	____________________
____________________	____________________
____________________	____________________

Do you know whether their firms have referred clients to your firm?

§ 7.02(f) Build a Biographical Information Base

Find out whether your firm has a data base that

captures marketing information. Also become familiar with its other data bases that can serve as marketing resources, particularly an automated conflicts of interest check system.

Create and build an information base of potential clients and referral sources; use it as a tool to assist you in maintaining contact with potential clients and referral sources. Collect information about their companies (and other business relationships) including: products/services, ownership, management team members, board of directors, the company's market share and competition, philosophy and culture, business goals, objectives, charitable organizations it supports, and so forth. *See* § 4.02 [Part I, Expectation No. 13: "Understand the Client's Business"]. In addition, obtain personal biographical information such as birthdays, children's names and ages, spouse, hobbies, boards, and civic organizations in which they are active. People are impressed when others remember personal interests they have shared; it demonstrates interest in the respective person and can go a long way toward creating the impression that you would also show interest in their legal matters.

§ 7.02(g) Leverage Your Speeches or Articles

When it becomes appropriate or expected that you write articles or deliver speeches, begin identifying subject matter of interest to existing and potential clients and referral source audiences (markets). Determine how to develop a topic into an article of significance to a specific client or referral market. Leverage your preparation time into multiple uses — that is, seek more than one audience for your presentation or article. For example, suppose you will make a presentation on the formation and start-up of a new business for a state bar institute. Determine to which additional nonlawyer groups the talk can be tailored with minimal additional work.

Topic	Initial Use	Other Uses
________________	________________	________________
________________	________________	________________

§ 7.02(h) Develop High Profile Involvement in an Organization

Another task in laying groundwork for future practice development is thoughtful selection of (or reevaluation of) memberships in civic organizations. Belonging to an organization, whether solely for personal enrichment or also for eventual client development, is a worthwhile use of your time only if you participate. Following a systematic process in researching and assessing options maximizes the likelihood that you will select organizations in whose objectives you are interested and in which your participation will become personally meaningful and eventually visible.

Factors to research about an organization include: its philosophy, goals, and recent accomplishments; its leadership, membership diversity, and turnover; the industry and business affiliations of its members; the opportunities it provides to build visibility; how much time you would have to commit; and so forth.

As you explore bar organizations and committees, assess how your participation can contribute to your marketing activities, as well as to your professional development and exchange of ideas and information. How would active involvement help you gain speaking engagements at CLE seminars, develop specialized expertise on the competitive edge of a practice area, generate referrals, and so forth?

Organization	Plan for Participation
______________	______________________________
	______________________________
______________	______________________________
	______________________________

§ 7.02(i) Improve Practical Knowledge of an Industry

List industries that your practice area targets for specific services. Find out what strategies are used to attract that business. For example, some firms have industry teams who focus on developing major accounts or entrepreneurial businesses in targeted industries and geographic locations.

Select a key industry and formulate a plan to become knowledgeable of its business practices and trends, companies with significant market share, trade associations, jargon, and so forth. *See* § 4.02 [Part I, Expectation No. 13: "Understand the Client's Business"]. Also become aware of pending legislation and innovations that will impact future business decisions and will create compliance problems. Identify legal/business problems that employers in the industry are facing. This research will serve as a tool to anticipate opportunities to develop expertise and clients in emerging specialty areas.

Industry: ______________________________

Acquaintances employed in that industry:

Name	Occupation	Title
____________	____________	____________
____________	____________	____________
____________	____________	____________

Sources of written data about the industry/client's business:

Data Sought	Source
________________________	____________
________________________	____________

§ 7.02(j) Use Firm Tools and Resources

Your firm may have developed a range of tools or resources for its members' use in marketing activities. Become acquainted with them and how they are effectively used. They may include:

Firm or practice area marketing plan

Brochures, capability packages

Data bases

Firm sponsored seminars

Articles

Press releases

Event tickets

Open houses

Community organization involvement opportunities

Announcements

Newsletters

Market research, surveys

APPLYING THIS EXPECTATION TO YOUR RESPONSIBILITIES

What marketing expectations, if any, does your firm have of each associate level?

You can lay groundwork to meet your firm's and your own expectations by:

Knowing your firm's key services and client markets.

Handling prospective client inquiries effectively.

Making a good first impression: every new acquaintance may become a potential client or referral source.

Developing relationships with counterparts in existing and potential client organizations.

Developing referral sources.

Identifying topics for articles and speeches of interest to clients and referral sources.

Leveraging your speeches and articles.

Developing meaningful involvement in an organization.

Building a biographical information data base.

Improving practical knowledge of a key industry's problems and trends using your firm's tools and resources.

Appendixes

APPENDIX A

While each firm has its own client new matter intake form, this form is intended for the Associate's own use as a checklist for amassing additional useful and necessary data that may be distributed throughout the client's files. This information, once gathered, can save time and effort in document preparation and research relative to the client's matter.

DETERMINING THE CLIENT'S NEEDS AND EXPECTATIONS

Attorney ______________________

Full Client Name ____________________ Date ________________

Client Address

Individual (contact) ______________________________________

Title ______________________________________

Company ______________________________________

Street ______________________________________

City ______________________________________

State ______________________ Zip ______________________

Billing Address

Individual ______________________________________

Title ______________________________________

Company ______________________________________

Street ______________________________

City ______________________________

State ______________ Zip ______________

Telephone Numbers

Office ______________________________

Car ______________________________

Residence ______________________________

Matter Name (to appear on computer files)

____

Matter Description ______________________________

Cross Reference File ______________________________

Source of Business (identify referral source, existing or former client, other) ______________________________

____

Client's Objective and Client's Evaluation of What is at Stake ______________________________

____

Business Context of Objective

____

____

Other Parties, Affiliations, etc. (conflicts data)

Name	Relationship
______________________	______________________
______________________	______________________
______________________	______________________
______________________	______________________
______________________	______________________
______________________	______________________

Major Facts, Assumptions

____

____

____

Problems, Constraints

____

____

____

Scope of Engagement

Lawyer's Responsibilities

____

____

____

Client's Responsibilities

____

____

____

Client Instructions and Special Handling Procedures

____

____

____

Pricing Arrangement and Estimate, Costs, Budgeting

Fee Arrangement ____________________________

Estimate __________________________________

Costs ____________________________________

Budgeting Notes ____________________________

Billing Procedures, Frequency, Format

____

____

Timeline Estimate

____

____

Action Plan Communicated to Client

____

____

Lead Lawyer's Team

____

____

____

Cross-Selling Opportunities and Timing ________________

____

APPENDIX B

COMMUNICATING EFFECTIVELY FROM THE CLIENT'S PERSPECTIVE

Can the client —

- Relate the value of your legal work to reaching the goal?
- Understand your strategy?
- Assess benefits and costs of alternative strategies or options — and make business decisions?
- Evaluate the effect of your efforts and timeline on other business plans?
- Perceive your billing (time) descriptions as relevant to the goal?

Does the client —

- Believe the matter is a priority to you?
- Perceive that you are accessible?
- Know what information you need from her/him — and by when?
- Understand the reason for a material change in timeline, cost or strategy? Did you present options to the supervising attorney or client (if appropriate)?
- Understand your correspondence and memoranda?
- Know your role and qualifications?
- Have confidence in your efforts?

Are you preparing the client to expect your next statement for professional services or will the client be surprised?

APPENDIX C

CLIENT SERVICE AUDIT

Corporate Counsel's Evaluation*

Client Contact ____________________

Title ____________________

Matter Evaluated ____________________

Responsible Attorney ____________________

Interviewer ____________________

Date ____________________

Client Attitude in Interview ____________________

Client's Overall Perception of Service (Excellent, good, fair, poor)

____

____

Client's Overall Perception of Firm's Strengths or Deficiencies

____

____

*This is intended as a checklist of items to address in an interview conducted by liaison or billing attorney. Another type of client survey is an anonymous survey conducted by mailed (or telephoned) questionnaire, in which the firm seeks to learn the perception of the firm held by the client base, rather than by individual clients.

Service Factors

Was responsible attorney/team sensitive to business goals and objectives? ________________________

____

Was client contact satisfied with: (Inquire about each factor and record comments)

Expertise/Confidence in Lawyer's Ability ________________

Result ____

Decision Making __________________________________

Problem Solving __________________________________

Budgeting ______________________________________

Staffing _______________________________________

Timetable ______________________________________

Accessibility of Responsible Attorney by telephone ________

Cost Consciousness _______________________________

Efficiency ______________________________________

Expected Technological Capabilities ___________________

Administrative Items ______________________________

Billing Method/Format _____________________________

Fees, Expenses __________________________________

Other ____

Other ____

Communication and Responsiveness

Did responsible attorney/team:

Consult with corporate counsel as expected?

____

Report status regularly and consult on course of action as expected? __________________________

Work as a team with the law department?

____

Return telephone calls promptly?

____

Confer re variations from original schedule or budget? __________________________

Did staff create and maintain a favorable impression? (at the firm, at the client's office, over the telephone, in correspondence, etc.)

____

Would client contact refer others to the responsible attorney? To the firm?

____

Client's comments that will assist in improving service:

____

____

What additional needs for legal services does client have/anticipate?

____

APPENDIX D

CHECKLIST OF ASSIGNMENT GROUND RULES

Purpose of assignment ____________________

Client's goal [clarified?] ____________________

Issues [clarified?] ____________________

Substantive facts, assumptions, guidelines [clarified?] __________

Tasks, sequencing [clarified?] ____________________

Immediate "To Do's" ____________________

Work product ____________________

Due date ____________________

Priority status ____________________

Interim reporting/review checkpoints [established?] __________

Time estimate and limitations ____________________

Special timekeeping, billing procedure ____________________

Special handling procedures ____________________

Sources for information ____________________

Firm resources ____________________

Authority to delegate ____________________

Expected client contact ____________________

  Purposes (gathering data/giving data) ____________________

  Names and titles of contacts ____________________

  Introduction (by contact attorney or self) ____________________

Expected contact with client's outside advisor(s) ____________________

Instructions for meeting preparation [clarified?] ____________________

APPENDIX E

CASE FLOW CHART

Updated: ______________________

Matter	Assignment Date	Priority Rank	Major Task	Major Task	Major Task	Date Due
			Start: Complete:	Start: Complete:	Start: Complete:	
			Start: Complete:	Start: Complete:	Start: Complete:	
			Start: Complete:	Start: Complete:	Start: Complete:	

APPENDIX F

TO DO LIST

Date: ______________________

A (Urgent)

Task	Time Estimated	Time Spent	Time Completed?
1.			
2.			
3.			
4.			
5.			

B (Important)

Task	Time Estimated	Time Spent	Time Completed?
1.			
2.			
3.			
4.			
5.			

C (Optional)

Task	Time Estimated	Time Spent	Time Completed?
1.			
2.			
3.			
4.			

Review at end of day —
Uncompleted items:

No.	A Complete by	No.	B Complete by	No.	C Complete by
____	____________	____	____________	____	____________
____	____________	____	____________	____	____________
____	____________	____	____________	____	____________

APPENDIX G

ASSIGNMENT MANAGEMENT WORKSHEET

Team:

Lead Attorney ______________________ Client ______________________

Other Attorneys ______________________ File No. ______________________

______________________ Matter ______________________

Legal Assistants ______________________

____

Your Project ____

____

Due Date ______________________

Major Tasks:*

Task No.	Task	Start By	Complete By	Report or Coordinate Person	Date

*Consider mapping out a complex project's major tasks on one worksheet and activities within a major task on a separate worksheet.

Number the tasks listed and use those numbers in a flow diagram.

Flow Diagram and Estimated Timeline:

APPENDIX H

WORKSHEET FOR MEETING PREPARATION

Date/Time of Meeting ______________________ Matter ______________________

Purpose: ____

Results/Actions to Accomplish: ______________________________________

____

Participants: ____

Length of Meeting: ____

Agenda:

Topic	Time Allocation
I. ______________________	______________________
A. ______________________	______________________
B. ______________________	______________________
II. ______________________	______________________
A. ______________________	______________________

B. ______________________ ______________________

III. ______________________ ______________________

A. ______________________ ______________________

B. ______________________ ______________________

IV. ______________________ ______________________

A. ______________________ ______________________

B. ______________________ ______________________

Participants	Role/Action

Follow-up/Next Step: ____

Table of Statutes, Rules, and Regulations

(References are to section numbers)

Federal Rules of Civil Procedure

Model Rules of Professional Conduct

Index of Subjects

(References are to section numbers)

C

D

E

F

G

H

I

J

L

M

Q

R

T

V

W

AILTO

A Comprehensive Resource
for ALL of Your In-House Training Needs

WHAT AILTO CAN DO FOR YOU

- Work with your office to determine your training needs
- Help your training committee design an effective training plan for your lawyers
- Provide your office with in-house training workshops on:
  - ⇒Associate Orientation
  - ⇒Legal Writing
  - ⇒Negotiating
  - ⇒Public Speaking
  - ⇒Interviewing and Counseling
  - ⇒Voice and Diction
  - ⇒Lawyer/Client Relations in the Corporate Setting*
  - ⇒Other Lawyering Skills
- Assist you in finding experts to present on-site seminars of all kinds
- Give you access to over 175 expert training consultants
- Offer you additional benefits and training support services through the AILTO membership program

AILTO in-house training workshops are taught by experts in the field of lawyer training. These programs are specifically tailored to the needs of your attorneys and the structure of your practice. Members of AILTO benefit from priority scheduling and special membership discounts on all AILTO in-house workshops. Nonmembers also may arrange for on-site delivery of these programs.

The American Institute for Law Training within the Office (AILTO) is a national, nonprofit organization that provides assistance and support to the in-house training efforts of law firms, law depart-

*Offered in conjunction with the Practising Law Institute

ments, and government agencies. Founded in 1985, AILTO is a project of the American Law Institute-American Bar Association Committee on Continuing Professional Education in cooperation with the American Bar Association Standing Committee on the Continuing Education of the Bar.

For more information about AILTO in-house training workshops and/or the AILTO membership program, write AILTO, 4025 Chestnut Street, Philadelphia, PA 19104 or call, toll-free, (800) CLE-NEWS, ext. 1614; in Pennsylvania (215) 243-1614.